Childcraft

The How and Why Library

Volume 1

Poems and Rhymes

Field Enterprises Educational Corporation

Chicago Frankfurt London Paris Rome Sydney Tokyo Toronto

1975 Edition

Childcraft—The How and Why Library

(Reg. U.S. Pat. Off.)

Acknowledgments

The publishers of *Childcraft—The How and Why Library* gratefully acknowledge the courtesy of the following publishers, agencies, corporations, and authors for permission to use copyrighted poems and illustrations. Full illustration acknowledgments for this volume appear on pages 308–309.

Abelard-Schuman, Limited: "Horses" from *Up the Windy Hill,* copyright 1953 by Aileen Fisher
Abingdon Press: "The Clock in the Hall" from *I Rode the Black Horse Far Away* by Ivy O. Eastwick, copyright © 1960 by Abingdon Press, this permission includes nonexclusive world rights
American Oil Company: art page 205
Atheneum Publishers: "Snowy Morning" by Lilian Moore, text copyright © 1969 by Lilian Moore, from *I Thought I Heard the City;* "The Toll Taker" by Patricia Hubbell, copyright © 1963 by Patricia Hubbell, from *The Apple Vendor's Fair;* "Toaster Time" by Eve Merriam, copyright © 1962 by Eve Merriam from *There Is No Rhyme for Silver;* used by permission of Atheneum Publishers
Baruch, Dorothy W.: "Stop—Go," "The Elevator," and "Merry-Go-Round" from *I Like Machinery,* copyright 1933 by Harper & Brothers
Boyden, Polly Chase: "Mud" from *Child Life*
Brandt & Brandt: "Afternoon on a Hill" from *Collected Poems* by Edna St. Vincent Millay, Harper & Brothers, copyright 1917, 1945 by Edna St. Vincent Millay; "Western Wagons" from *A Book of Americans,* Rinehart & Company, Inc., copyright 1933 by Rosemary and Stephen Vincent Benét
Brown, Ltd., Curtis: "Jonathan Bing" from *Jonathan Bing and Other Verses,* by Beatrice Curtis Brown, copyright 1936 by Beatrice Curtis Brown
Burgess, Gelett: "The Purple Cow" from *The Burgess Nonsense Book*
Cape, Limited, Jonathan: "Leisure" from *Collected Poems* by William Henry Davies, reprinted by permission of Mrs. H. M. Davies
Chaffee, Eleanor A.: "The Cobbler"
Children's Activities magazine publishers: "A New Friend" by Marjorie Allen Anderson
The Cream of Wheat Corp.: photo by Carroll Seghers II, page 92, copyright The Cream of Wheat Corp.
Cullen, Mrs. Ida M.: "Song of the Wake-Up-World" by Countee Cullen
Davies, Mary Carolyn: "Drums of the Rain" and "Look at the Snow" from *Child Life*
Day Company, Inc., The John: "Skyscraper Is a City's House" from *Skyscraper* by Elsa Naumburg, Clara Lambert, and Lucy Sprague Mitchell, copyright 1933 by The John Day Company, Inc.
Dodd, Mead & Company: "The World" by William Brighty Rands; "Two Cats of Kilkenny" from *The Little Mother Goose,* compiled by Jessie Wilcox Smith
Doubleday & Company, Inc.: "The Best Game the Fairies Play" from *Fairies and Chimneys* by Rose Fyleman, copyright 1920 by Doubleday & Company, Inc.; "Good Night," "Hippopotamus," "Mice," and "Sneezes" from *Fifty-One New Nursery Rhymes* by Rose Fyleman, copyright 1932 by Doubleday & Company, Inc.; "The Dentist," "Joys," "My Policeman," and "Singing Time" from *The Fairy Green* by Rose Fyleman, copyright 1923 by Doubleday & Company, Inc.; "The New Neighbor" and "October" from *Gay Go Up* by Rose Fyleman, copyright 1930 by Doubleday & Company, Inc., all by courtesy Society of Authors; "Rain in the Night" from *Selected Lyrics* by Amelia Josephine Burr, copyright 1927 by Doubleday & Company, Inc.; "The Animal Store," "Barefoot Days," "Good Green Bus," "The Ice-Cream Man," "I'd Like To Be a Lighthouse," and "Taxis" from *Taxis and Toadstools* by Rachel Field, copyright 1926 by Doubleday & Company, Inc.; "Sunrise" by Katherine Kosmak from *Creative Youth,* edited by Hughes Mearns, copyright 1925 by Doubleday & Company, Inc.; second stanza of "Miss Norma Jean Pugh, First Grade Teacher" from *People I'd Like to Keep,* copyright © 1964 by Mary O'Neill, reprinted by permission of Doubleday & Company, Inc., courtesy World's Work Ltd.; "Country Trucks" from *Goose Grass Rhymes* by Monica Shannon, copyright 1930 by Doubleday & Company, Inc.
Dutton & Co., Inc., E. P.: "Bridges," "Galoshes," and "Stars" from the book *Stories To Begin On* by Rhoda W. Bacmeister, copyright 1940 by E. P. Dutton & Co., Inc., renewal © 1968 by Rhoda W. Bacmeister; "Dogs," "Drinking Fountain," "In Winter," and "Sliding," copyright 1946 by Marchette Chute; "In August," copyright 1941 by Marchette Chute; and "My Dog," copyright 1932 by Marchette Chute and "Spring Rain," copyright 1946 by Marchette Chute, from the book *Around and About,* copyright 1932 by Marchette Chute, published 1957 by E. P. Dutton & Co., Inc.; "Food" and "Mail" from the book *Rhymes About the City* by Marchette Chute, copyright 1946 by Marchette Chute; "Shadow Dance" from the book *Fairies and Suchlike* by Ivy O. Eastwick, copyright 1946 by E. P. Dutton & Co., Inc.; "When I Get Into Bed," from the book *Youngsters* by Burges Johnson, copyright 1921 by E. P. Dutton & Co., Inc., renewal, 1949, by Burges Johnson, published by E. P. Dutton & Co., Inc.; "The End," "Forgiven," and "Furry Bear" from the book *Now We Are Six* by A. A. Milne, copyright 1927 by E. P. Dutton & Co., Inc., renewal 1955 by A. A. Milne, courtesy Methuen & Co., Ltd.; "Halfway Down," "Hoppity," "Puppy and I," "Spring Morning," and "Vespers" from the book *When We Were Very Young* by A. A. Milne, copyright 1924 by E. P. Dutton & Co., Inc., renewal 1952 by A. A. Milne, courtesy Methuen & Co., Ltd.; "Jump or Jiggle" by Evelyn Beyer, "Little Black Bug" by Margaret Wise Brown, "The House of the Mouse" by Lucy Sprague Mitchell from *Another Here and Now Story Book,* compiled by Lucy Sprague Mitchell, copyright 1937 by E. P. Dutton & Co., Inc.; reprinted with permission
Eastwick, Ivy O.: "From the Sky" and "Moon-in-Water," courtesy Ivy O. Eastwick; "May Mornings" reprinted by special permission from *Jack and Jill*
Edelman, Katherine: "Saturday Shopping" from *Child Life*
Fallis, Edwina H.: "September" from *Sung Under the Silver Umbrella*
Farrar, Straus & Giroux, Inc.: "mommies" from *Spin A Soft Black Song* by Nikki Giovanni, copyright © 1971 by Nikki Giovanni, reprinted with the permission of Farrar, Straus & Giroux, Inc.
The First-Stamford National Bank & Trust Company, Stamford, Connecticut: "Dogs and Weather" by Winifred Welles from *Skipping Along Alone*
Fisher, Aileen: "After a Bath" and "Shelling Peas" from *Inside a Little House;* "Otherwise" from *The Coffee-Pot Face;* "December," from *That's Why*
Flexman, J.: "The Shiny Little House" by Nancy M. Hayes
Follett Publishing Company: "Motor Cars" by Rowena Bastin Bennett from *Around a Toadstool Table,* copyright 1930, 1937 by Follett Publishing Company, Chicago, Illinois; "Rubber Boots" and "A Modern Dragon" from *Songs Around a Toadstool Table,* copyright © 1967 by Rowena Bennett, copyright © 1930, 1937 by Follett Publishing Company. Used by permission of Follett Publishing Company, division of Follett Corporation
French, Inc., Samuel: "Washing" by John Drinkwater from the book *More About Me,* copyright first impressions October 1929, copyright second impressions November 1929
Frost, Frances: "Sniff" from *American Junior Red Cross News*
Fyleman, Rose: "The Beech Tree" from *Child Life*
Guiterman, Mrs. Arthur: "Chums" by Arthur Guiterman from *Child Life*
Harcourt Brace Jovanovich, Inc.: Haiku by Boncho, Chiyo, and Shiki from *Cricket Songs: Japanese Haiku,* translated and © 1964 by Harry Behn, reprinted by permission of Harcourt Brace Jovanovich, Inc., and Curtis Brown, Ltd.; "Circles" and "Trees" from *The Little Hill* by Harry Behn, copyright 1949 by Harry Behn; "The Merry-Go-Round" and "Sliding" from *Whispers and Other Poems,* © 1958 by Myra Cohn Livingston; "Bump on My Knee" from *Wide Awake and Other Poems,* © 1959 by Myra Cohn Livingston; "Spring Wind," "When Young Melissa Sweeps," and "Wings and Wheels" from *Magpie Lane* by Nancy Byrd Turner, copyright 1927 by Harcourt, Brace & Company, Inc., renewed 1955 by Nancy Byrd Turner; photographs from *The Shadow Book* by Beatrice Schenk de Regniers; photographs copyright 1960 by Isabel Gordon, pages 82 and 83 (*left, top and bottom right*); reproduced and reprinted by permission of publisher
Harper & Row, Publishers: "The Mitten Song" and "My Zipper Suit" from *A Pocketful of Rhymes* by Marie Louise Allen, copyright 1939 by Harper & Brothers; "Rudolph Is Tired of the City," "Tommy," and "Vern" from *Bronzeville Boys and Girls* by Gwendolyn Brooks, copyright © 1956 by Gwendolyn Brooks Blakely; first verse of "Counting" and "The Rose on my Cake" from *The Rose on my Cake* by Karla Kuskin, copyright © 1964 by Karla Kuskin; "Little Seeds We Sow In Spring" from *The Winds That Come From Faraway* by Else Holmelund Minarik, copyright © 1964 by Else Holmelund Minarik; "Building a Skyscraper" and "Sleet Storm" from *A World To Know* by James S. Tippett, copyright 1933 by Harper & Brothers; "Sh" from *I Live in a City* by James S. Tippett, copyright 1927 by Harper & Brothers, 1955 by James S. Tippett; "Engine," "Ferry-Boats," and "Up in the Air" from *I Go A-Traveling* by James S. Tippett, copyright 1929 Harper

& Brothers, renewed 1957 James S. Tippett; reprinted with permission of Harper & Row, Publishers

Head, Cloyd: "Moving" and "Thaw" by Eunice Tietjens

Heath & Company, D. C.: "Trains at Night" by Frances Frost from *The Packet*

Henry Holt and Company, Inc.: "The Pasture" from *Complete Poems of Robert Frost*, copyright 1930, 1949 by Henry Holt and Company, Inc., courtesy Pearn, Pollinger and Higham, Ltd. and Jonathan Cape, Ltd.; "Fog" from *Chicago Poems* by Carl Sandburg, copyright 1916 by Henry Holt and Company, Inc., 1944 by Carl Sandburg; "Chick, Chick Chatterman," "I Had a Cow," and "I Know a Man" from *A Rocket In My Pocket,* compiled by Carl Withers

Houghton Mifflin Company: "The Sun" by John Drinkwater from *All About Me;* "Dandelions" by Frances Frost from *Pool In the Meadow;* "The Snowbird" by Frank Dempster Sherman from *Little Folk Lyrics*

Hughes, Langston: "City," and "Garment," from an anthology *Golden Slippers,* compiled by Arna Bontemps

The Instructor Publications, Inc.: "When I'm an Astronaut" by Leland B. Jacobs from *The Instructor,* © The Instructor Publications, Inc.

Jaques, Florence Page: "There Once Was a Puffin"

Johnson, Dorothy Vena: "Palace" from an anthology *Golden Slippers,* compiled by Arna Bontemps

Keller, Mark C.: "Little Joe Tunney" by Rebecca McCann

Knopf, Inc., Alfred A.: "The Elephant" and "The Vulture" from *Bad Child's Book of Beasts* by Hilaire Belloc, courtesy Gerald Duckworth and Co., Ltd.; "In Time of Silver Rain" from "In Time of Silver Rain," copyright 1938 and renewed 1966 by Langston Hughes, reprinted from *Fields of Wonder,* by Langston Hughes, by permission of Alfred A. Knopf, Inc.; "Snail" from *Fields of Wonder* by Langston Hughes, copyright 1947 by Langston Hughes

Lerner Publications Company: "Happy Birthday" from *Swing Around the Sun* by Barbara Justen Esbensen, copyright © 1965 Lerner Publications Company, Minneapolis

Lippincott Company, J. B.: "How to Tell the Top of a Hill" and "The River Is a Piece of Sky" from the book *The Reason for the Pelican* by John Ciardi, copyright © 1959 by John Ciardi. Reprinted by permission of J. B. Lippincott Company; "Mouse" from *Poems for a Little Girl* by Hilda Conkling, copyright 1920, 1947 by Hilda Conkling; "City Streets and Country Roads" from *Joan's Door* by Eleanor Farjeon, copyright 1926 by J. B. Lippincott Company; "Choosing" from *Poems for Children* by Eleanor Farjeon, copyright 1933, 1961 by Eleanor Farjeon, published by J. B. Lippincott Company, courtesy David Higham Associates, Ltd.; "A Kitten" and "Mrs. Peck-Pigeon" from *Over the Garden Wall* by Eleanor Farjeon, copyright 1933, 1951 by Eleanor Farjeon; "We Are All Nodding" from *Four and Twenty Blackbirds,* collected by Helen Dean Fish, copyright 1937 by J. B. Lippincott Company; "Jonathan" from *Picture Rhymes from Foreign Lands,* collected by Rose Fyleman, copyright 1935 by Rose Fyleman, courtesy Society of Authors; "E Is the Escalator" and "P's the Proud Policeman" from *All Around the Town* by Phyllis McGinley, copyright 1948 by McGinley, courtesy Curtis Brown, Ltd.; "Song for a Little House" from *Chimneysmoke* by Christopher Morley, copyright 1917, 1945 by Christopher Morley, courtesy Christopher Morley; "Animal Crackers" from *Songs for a Little House* by Christopher Morley, copyright 1917, 1945 by Christopher Morley, courtesy Christopher Morley; "Indian Children," "A Letter Is a Gypsy Elf," and "The Telegraph" from the book *For Days and Days* by Annette Wynne, copyright 1919 by J. B. Lippincott Company, renewal 1947 by Annette Wynne, reprinted by permission of the publishers

Little, Brown and Co.: "Five Chants—Part I," "Song of the Train," and "This is my Rock" from *Far and Few* by David McCord, copyright 1952 by David McCord, by permission of Little, Brown and Co.

Long, Elizabeth-Ellen: "Autumn Song," reprinted by special permission from *Jack and Jill*

Lynde, Mary Ellen: "Queen Anne's Lace" by Mary Leslie Newton, courtesy *The New York Times*

The Macmillan Company: "Skating" by Herbert Asquith from *Pillicock Hill,* courtesy William Heinemann, Ltd.; "The Light-Hearted Fairy" from *Gaily We Parade,* selected by John E. Brewton; "Mr. Nobody" from *Bridled with Rainbows,* edited by Sara and John E. Brewton; "The Kangaroo," "Sea Gull," "Song," and "The Ways of Trains" from *Summer Green* by Elizabeth Coatsworth; "November" from *Twelve Months Make a Year* by Elizabeth Coatsworth; "Something Told the Wild Geese" from *Branches Green* by Rachel Field; "A Summer Morning" from *The Pointed People* by Rachel Field; "An Explanation of the Grasshopper," "The Little Turtle," and "The Mysterious Cat" from *Collected Poems* by Vachel Lindsay; "Bees," "The Hummingbird," and "Toucans Two" reprinted with permission of Macmillan Publishing Co., Inc. from *Toucans Two and Other Poems* by Jack Prelutsky, copyright © 1967, 1970 by Jack Prelutsky, courtesy Hamish Hamilton Children's Books Ltd.; "Breakfast Time" from *Collected Poems* by James Stephens, courtesy The Macmillan Company, Ltd., and James Stephens; "April" from *Collected Poems* by Sara Teasdale; "February Twilight" from *February Twilight* by Sara Teasdale, copyright 1934 by The Macmillan Company; "Falling Star" from *Stars Tonight* by Sara Teasdale

McDonald, Jessica Nelson North: "Three Guests" by Jessica Nelson North

McKay Company, David: "Road Fellows" from *Christopher O!* by Barbara Young, copyright 1947 by Barbara Young

McKay, Lois W.: "Night" from *Child Life*

McWebb, Elizabeth Upham: "At Mrs. Appleby's"

Meigs, Mildred Plew: "Pirate Don Durk of Dowdee"

Miller, Mary Britton: "Cat" and "Shore" from *Menagerie*

Mitchell, Mrs. Alec: "Walking" by Grace Glaubitz from *The Golden Flute,* compiled by Alice Hubbard and Adeline Babbit

Monro, Alida: "Overheard on a Saltmarsh" from *Children of Love* by Harold Monro

John Murray (Publishers) Ltd.: "Under the willow—" from *The Autumn Wind, Wisdom of the East Series* translated by Lewis Mackenzie

Newsome, Effie Lee: "Quoits" from *Golden Slippers*

Ober, Harold Associates, Incorporated: "Cycle" copyright 1941 by Langston Hughes, renewed, from *Golden Slippers.* Reprinted by permission of Harold Ober Associates Incorporated

Oxford University Press (London Office): "Down with the Lambs" from *The Oxford Nursery Rhyme Book,* edited by Iona and Peter Opie, Oxford University Press, Inc., 1955

Pageant Press: "Alone by the Surf" by Leila Kendall Brown from *A Little Child Looking,* copyright 1956 by Pageant Press

Pantheon Books, Inc.: "Horsies Make Horsies" by John Leonard Becker from *New Feathers from the Old Goose,* copyright 1956 by Pantheon Books, Inc.; "Who Is So Pretty?" from *Mouse Chorus* by Elizabeth Coatsworth, copyright 1955 by Pantheon Books, Inc.

Pierce, Dorothy Mason: "Sprinkling" by Dorothy Mason Pierce from *Sung Under the Silver Umbrella*

Putnam's Sons, G. P. & Coward-McCann, Inc.: "Everybody Says," "Like Me," "My Nose," and "The Reason" from *All Together* by Dorothy Aldis, copyright 1925, 1926, 1927, 1928, 1929, 1939, 1952 by Dorothy Aldis; "Brooms," "Hiding," "Ice," "Little," "Naughty Soap Song," and "Winter" from *Everything and Anything* by Dorothy Aldis, copyright 1925, 1926, 1927 by Dorothy Aldis; "About Buttons" from *Here, There and Everywhere* by Dorothy Aldis, copyright 1927, 1928 by Dorothy Aldis; "Names" and "The Picnic" from *Hop, Skip and Jump* by Dorothy Aldis, copyright 1934 by Dorothy Aldis

Rand McNally & Co.: "The Cricket" by Marjorie Barrows; "Swimming" by Clinton Scollard from *Child Life Magazine,* copyright 1923, 1951 by Rand McNally & Co.

Richards, The Estate of Laura E.: "The Cave Boy" by Laura E. Richards from *Child Life*

Sidgwick & Jackson, Ltd.: "Choosing Shoes" from *The Very Thing* by Ffrida Wolfe

Smithsonian Institution: Chippewa poem from *Chippewa Music* translated by Frances Densmore, Bureau of American Ethnology Bulletin 53, 1913

The Society of Authors: "Miss T" from *Selected Poems;* "The Cupboard," "Some One," and "Summer Evening," by Walter de la Mare, granted by The Literary Trustees of Walter de la Mare and the Society of Aut   as their representative

Stern, Mrs. David: "Holding Hands" by Lenore M. Link, from *Arbuthnot Anthology of Children's Literature*

Stiles, Dr. Lindley J.: "Growing" from *Moods and Moments* by L. J. Stiles

Story Parade, Inc.: "Kite Days" by Mark Sawyer from *Story Parade,* copyright 1939 by Story Parade, Inc.

Thompson, Dorothy Brown: "Maps" from *Bridled with Rainbows,* selected by Sara and John E. Brewton; and "Bigger" from the anthology *For A Child*

Time, Inc.: photography by Alfred Eisenstaedt, page 83 (center), courtesy *Life,* copyright 1959 by Time, Inc.

Turner, Nancy Byrd: "Wind Capers" from *Child Life*

Untermeyer, Mrs. Jean Starr: "Glimpse in Autumn" by Jean Starr Untermeyer from *This Singing World,* edited by Louis Untermeyer

Vanada, Lillian Schulz: "Fuzzy Wuzzy, Creepy Crawly" by Lillian Schulz

The Viking Press, Inc.: "The Prayer of the Little Bird" from *Prayers from the Ark* by Carmen Bernos de Gasztold, trans. by Rumer Godden, copyright © by Rumer Godden, courtesy Macmillan and Company, Ltd. and Rumer Godden; "Baby Goat" from *Jingle Jangle* by Zhenya Gay, copyright 1953 by Zhenya Gay; "The Little House" from *Green Outside* by Elizabeth Godley, copyright 1932 by The Viking Press, Inc., courtesy Oxford University Press; "Firefly," "Mumps," "The Rabbit," "The Woodpecker," from *Under the Tree* by Elizabeth Madox Roberts, copyright 1922 by B. W. Heubsch, Inc., 1950 by Ivor S. Roberts; "Shoes" from *In and Out* by Tom Robinson, copyright 1943 by Tom Robinson

John Weatherhill, Inc.: "A Dream Party" and "The Song of the Frog" from *The Prancing Pony, Nursery Rhymes from Japan* adapted into English by Charlotte B. DeForest, copyright 1967 by John Weatherhill, Inc.

Willson, Dixie: "The Mist and All" from *Child Life*

Winston Company, The John C.: "An Indignant Male" by Abram Bunn Ross from *Five Going on Six*

Wood, Ray: "Fishy-Fishy in the Brook," "Had a Mule," "Hush, My Baby," and "Seven Blackbirds in a Tree" from *The American Mother Goose,* collected by Ray Wood

Worth, Kathryn: "Smells" from *Poems for Josephine*

Preface

Childcraft was first published in 1934. Since then it has undergone substantial revision several times. This edition is a 15-volume resource library designed especially for preschool and primary-grade children and for the older child who needs high-interest, easy-to-read materials. *Childcraft* also serves as a resource for parents, teachers, and librarians.

Outstanding educational and child guidance specialists serve on the Childcraft Editorial Advisory Board. This group works with the editors and artists in selecting and preparing the contents of these volumes. *Childcraft* concentrates on broad areas of children's interests that have been identified through research and direct observation of children.

In addition, *Childcraft* relates to broad areas of the school curriculum. Volumes 1, 2, and 3 relate to Literature and the Language Arts; Volumes 4, 5, 6, and 7 to Science; Volumes 8, 9, and 10 to Social Studies; Volumes 11, 12, and 13 to Creative Activities and Fine Arts; and Volume 14 to Health and Safety. Of course, Volume 15 is designed primarily to serve parents and teachers.

Throughout *Childcraft*, easy-to-read text is combined with appealing illustrations that make the material not only fun to read, but also fun to look at. Nearly every graphic technique appears somewhere in *Childcraft*. The illustrators include many of the world's top-ranking artists and photographers, including all of the winners of the Caldecott Medal, awarded annually by a committee of children's librarians for the most distinguished picture book for children. Color is used throughout the set, both to capture interest and to inform.

Childcraft is designed to encourage the young child to open doors to life and learning. The volumes also help start the child on a lifelong adventure of enrichment through books. For more information on using *Childcraft* effectively, see Volume 15.

The Editors and Artists

Volume 1

Poems and Rhymes

Contents

Old Mother Goose, when
She wanted to wander,
Would fly through the air
On a very fine gander.

HUSH-A-BYE, BABY

Hush-a-bye, baby, on the tree top,
When the wind blows the cradle will rock;
When the bough breaks the cradle will fall,
Down will come baby, cradle, and all.

HUSH, LITTLE BABY

Hush, little baby, don't say a word,
Papa's going to buy you a mockingbird.

If the mockingbird won't sing,
Papa's going to buy you a diamond ring.

If the diamond ring turns to brass,
Papa's going to buy you a looking glass.

If the looking glass gets broke,
Papa's going to buy you a billy goat.

If that billy goat runs away,
Papa's going to buy you another today.

BYE, BABY BUNTING

Bye, baby bunting,
Daddy's gone a-hunting,
Gone to get a rabbit skin
To wrap the baby bunting in.

SWEETER THAN SUGAR

My little baby, little boy blue,
Is as sweet as sugar and cinnamon too;
Isn't this precious darling of ours
Sweeter than dates and cinnamon flowers?

PAT-A-CAKE

Pat-a-cake, pat-a-cake,
  Baker's man,
Bake me a cake
  As fast as you can.
Pat it and prick it,
  And mark it with a B,
And put it in the oven
  For baby and me.

PEASE PORRIDGE HOT

Pease porridge hot,
  Pease porridge cold,
Pease porridge in the pot,
  Nine days old.
Some like it hot,
  Some like it cold,
Some like it in the pot,
  Nine days old.

RIDE A COCKHORSE

Ride a cockhorse to Banbury Cross,
  To see a fine lady upon a white horse.
With rings on her fingers,
  And bells on her toes,
She shall have music wherever she goes.

THIS IS THE WAY THE LADIES RIDE

This is the way the ladies ride,
  Tri, tre, tre, tree, tri, tre, tre, tree!
This is the way the ladies ride,
  Tri, tre, tre, tree, tri, tre, tre, tree!

This is the way the gentlemen ride,
  Gallop-a-trot, gallop-a-trot!
This is the way the gentlemen ride,
  Gallop-a-gallop-a-trot!

This is the way the farmers ride,
  Hobbledy-hoy, hobbledy-hoy!
This is the way the farmers ride,
  Hobbledy-hobbledy-hoy!

RING-A-RING O' ROSES

Ring-a-ring o' roses,
A pocket full of posies,
  A-tishoo! A-tishoo!
We all fall down.

JACK BE NIMBLE

Jack be nimble,
    Jack be quick,
Jack jump over
    The candlestick.

HAD A MULE

Had a mule, his name was Jack,
    I rode his tail to save his back;
His tail got loose and I fell back—
    Whoa, Jack!

ONE, TWO,
BUCKLE MY SHOE

One, two,
Buckle my shoe;

Three, four,
Knock at the door;

Five, six,
Pick up sticks;

Seven, eight,
Lay them straight;

Nine, ten,
A good fat hen.

ONE,
TWO,
THREE,
FOUR,
FIVE

One, two, three, four, five!
I caught a hare alive;
Six, seven, eight, nine, ten!
I let her go again.

SNEEZES

One sneeze is lucky,
Two sneezes queer,
Three sneezes—get your hanky
(Oh, dear, dear),
Four sneezes—off she goes
Into her bed and under the clo'es.

ROSE FYLEMAN

16

SEVEN BLACKBIRDS IN A TREE

Seven blackbirds in a tree,
Count them and see what they be.
One for sorrow
Two for joy
Three for a girl
Four for a boy;
Five for silver
Six for gold
Seven for a secret
That's never been told.

THIS LITTLE PIG WENT TO MARKET

This little pig went to market,
This little pig stayed at home,
This little pig had roast beef,
This little pig had none,
And this little pig cried,
    "Wee-wee-wee-wee-wee,
I can't find my way home."

WHAT ARE LITTLE BOYS MADE OF?

What are little boys made of, made of?
What are little boys made of?
    Frogs and snails
    And puppy-dogs' tails,
That's what little boys are made of.

What are little girls made of, made of?
What are little girls made of?
    Sugar and spice
    And all things nice,
That's what little girls are made of.

JACK AND JILL

Jack and Jill went up the hill,
To fetch a pail of water;
Jack fell down and broke his crown,
And Jill came tumbling after.

Then up Jack got and home did trot,
As fast as he could caper.
He went to bed to mend his head
With vinegar and brown paper.

MARY, MARY, QUITE CONTRARY

Mary, Mary, quite contrary,
How does your garden grow?
With cockleshells, and silver bells,
And pretty maids all in a row.

GEORGY PORGY

Georgy Porgy, pudding and pie,
Kissed the girls and made them cry;
When the boys came out to play,
Georgy Porgy ran away.

We are all nodding, nid, nid, nodding,
We are all nodding
At our house at home.
With a turning in and a turning out,
And it's this way, that way, round about,
We are all nodding, nid, nid, nodding,
We are all nodding
At our house at home.

WE ARE ALL NODDING

We are all sewing, sew, sew, sewing,
We are all sewing
At our house at home.
With a turning in and a turning out,
And it's this way, that way, round about,
We are all sewing, sew, sew, sewing,
We are all sewing
At our house at home.

We are all fiddling, fid, fid, fiddling,
We are all fiddling
At our house at home.
With a turning in and a turning out,
And it's this way, that way, round about,
We are all fiddling, fid, fid, fiddling,
We are all fiddling
At our house at home.

We are all reading, read, read, reading,
We are all reading
At our house at home.
With a turning in and a turning out,
And it's this way, that way, round about,
We are all reading, read, read, reading,
We are all reading
At our house at home.

We are all spinning, spin, spin, spinning,
We are all spinning
At our house at home.
With a turning in and a turning out,
And it's this way, that way, round about,
We are all spinning, spin, spin, spinning,
We are all spinning
At our house at home.

HUMPTY DUMPTY
SAT ON
A WALL

Humpty Dumpty sat on a wall,
Humpty Dumpty had a great fall;
All the King's horses and all the King's men
Couldn't put Humpty Dumpty together again.

24   An Egg

AS I WAS GOING TO ST. IVES

As I was going to St. Ives,
I met a man with seven wives;
Each wife had seven sacks,
Each sack had seven cats,
Each cat had seven kits.
Kits, cats, sacks, and wives,
How many were going to St. Ives?

One

AS WHITE
AS MILK

As white as milk,
As soft as silk,
And hundreds close together;
They sail away
On an autumn day,
When windy is the weather.

WILHELMINA SEEGMILLER

Milkweed Seed

LITTLE NANCY ETTICOAT

Little Nancy Etticoat,
In a white petticoat,
And a red nose.
The longer she stands,
The shorter she grows.

A Candle

THIRTY WHITE HORSES

Thirty white horses
On a red hill;
Now they tramp,
Now they champ,
Now they stand still.

The Teeth and Gums

LITTLE BO-PEEP

Little Bo-Peep has lost her sheep
   And can't tell where to find them;
Leave them alone, and they'll come home,
   Wagging their tails behind them.

Little Bo-Peep fell fast asleep,
   And dreamed she heard them bleating.
But when she awoke, she found it a joke.
   For still they all were fleeting.

Then she took her little crook,
   Determined for to find them;
She found them indeed, but it made her heart bleed,
   For they'd left their tails behind them.

It happened one day, as Bo-Peep did astray
   Unto a meadow hard by,
There she espied their tails, side by side,
   All hung on a tree to dry.

She heaved a sigh and wiped her eye,
   And ran o'er hill and dale,
And tried what she could, as a shepherdess should,
   To tack each sheep to its tail.

MARY HAD A LITTLE LAMB

Mary had a little lamb,
  Its fleece was white as snow;
And everywhere that Mary went
  The lamb was sure to go.

He followed her to school one day;
  That was against the rule;
It made the children laugh and play
  To see a lamb at school.

SARAH JOSEPHA HALE

PUSSYCAT, PUSSYCAT

Pussycat, pussycat, where have you been?
I've been to London to look at the Queen.
Pussycat, pussycat, what did you there?
I frightened a little mouse under the chair.

JONATHAN

Jonathan Gee
  Went out with his cow;
    He climbed up a tree
    And sat on a bough.
      He sat on a bough
        And broke it in half,
          And John's old cow
    Did nothing but laugh.

ROSE FYLEMAN

LITTLE BOY BLUE

Little Boy Blue, come blow your horn;
The sheep's in the meadow, the cow's in the corn.
Where's the little boy that looks after the sheep?
He's under the haystack, fast asleep.

LITTLE
MISS MUFFET

Little Miss Muffet
  Sat on a tuffet,
Eating of curds and whey;
  Along came a spider,
  And sat down beside her,
  And frightened Miss Muffet away.

THREE LITTLE KITTENS

Three little kittens lost their mittens,
And they began to cry,
"Oh, mother dear,
We very much fear
That we have lost our mittens."

"Lost your mittens!
You naughty kittens!
Then you shall have no pie."
"Mee-ow, mee-ow, mee-ow."
"No, you shall have no pie."

The three little kittens found their mittens,
And they began to cry,
"Oh, mother dear,
See here, see here!
See, we have found our mittens."

"Put on your mittens,
You silly kittens,
And you shall have some pie."
"Purr-r, purr-r, purr-r.
Oh, let us have the pie!
Purr-r, purr-r, purr-r."

The three little kittens put on their mittens,
And soon ate up the pie.
"Oh, mother dear,
We greatly fear
That we have soiled our mittens!"

"Soiled your mittens!
You naughty kittens!"
Then they began to sigh,
"Mee-ow, mee-ow, mee-ow."
Then they began to sigh,
"Mee-ow, mee-ow, mee-ow."

The three little kittens washed their mittens,
And hung them up to dry.
"Oh, mother dear,
Do you not hear
That we have washed our mittens?"

"Washed your mittens!
Oh, you're good kittens,
But I smell a rat close by.

Hush! hush! Mee-ow, mee-ow."
"We smell a rat close by,
Mee-ow, mee-ow, mee-ow."

TO MARKET, TO MARKET

To market, to market,
To buy a fat pig,
Home again, home again,
Jiggety-jig.

To market, to market,
To buy a fat hog,
Home again, home again,
Jiggety-jog.

To market, to market,
To buy a plum bun,
Home again, home again,
Market is done.

HIGGLEDY, PIGGLEDY,
MY BLACK HEN

Higgledy, piggledy, my black hen,
She lays eggs for gentlemen;
Gentlemen come every day
To see what my black hen doth lay.

BAA, BAA, BLACK SHEEP

Baa, Baa, black sheep,
Have you any wool?
Yes sir, yes sir,
Three bags full:

One for my master,
And one for my dame,
And one for the little boy
Who lives in the lane.

LITTLE
ROBIN
REDBREAST

Little Robin Redbreast sat upon a tree;
Up went Pussycat, and down went he.
Down came Pussycat, and away Robin ran;
Said little Robin Redbreast, "Catch me if you can."

Little Robin Redbreast jumped upon a wall;
Pussycat jumped after him, and almost got a fall.
Little Robin chirped and sang, and what did Pussy say?
Pussycat said naught but "Mew," and Robin flew away.

ONCE I SAW A
LITTLE BIRD

Once I saw a little bird
Come hop, hop, hop;
So I cried, "Little bird,
Will you stop, stop, stop?"
I was going to the window
To say, "How do you do?"
But he shook his little tail,
And far away he flew.

CHICK, CHICK,
CHATTERMAN

Chick, chick, chatterman
　　How much are your geese?
Chick, chick, chatterman
　　Five cents apiece.
Chick, chick, chatterman
　　That's too dear.
Chick, chick, chatterman
　　Get out of here.

HEY, DIDDLE, DIDDLE

Hey, diddle, diddle!
  The cat and the fiddle,
The cow jumped over the moon;
  The little dog laughed
  To see such sport,
And the dish ran away with the spoon.

COCK-A-DOODLE-DOO

Cock-a-doodle-doo!
My dame has lost her shoe.
My master's lost his fiddling stick,
And doesn't know what to do!

Cock-a-doodle-doo!
What is my dame to do?
Till master finds his fiddling stick,
She'll dance without her shoe.

I HAD A COW

I had a cow that gave such milk
I dressed her in the finest silk;
I fed her on the finest hay,
And milked her twenty times a day.

TWO CATS OF KILKENNY

There once were two cats of Kilkenny,
Each thought there was one cat too many;
So they fought and they fit,
And they scratched and they bit,
Till, excepting their nails
And the tips of their tails,
Instead of two cats, there weren't any.

HIPPOPOTAMUS

Hi, hippopotamus, hip, hip, hip!
What an ugly face you've got,
what an ugly lip;
Can't you come and play a bit,
dance and hop and skip?
Come, hippopotamus, hip, hip, hip!

ROSE FYLEMAN

FISHY-FISHY
IN THE BROOK

Fishy-fishy in the brook
Daddy caught him with a hook;
Mammy fried him in the pan
And baby ate him like a man.

THE OLD WOMAN IN THE SHOE

There was an old woman who lived in a shoe.
She had so many children she didn't know what to do.
She gave them some broth, without any bread,
She spanked them all soundly, and sent them to bed.

THERE WAS AN OLD WOMAN

There was an old woman
Lived under a hill,
And if she's not gone,
She lives there still.

PETER, PETER, PUMPKIN-EATER

Peter, Peter, pumpkin-eater,
Had a wife and couldn't keep her;
He put her in a pumpkin shell,
And there he kept her very well.

SIMPLE SIMON

Simple Simon met a pieman,
  Going to the fair;
Says Simple Simon to the pieman,
  "Let me taste your ware."

Says the pieman unto Simon,
  "Show me first your penny."
Says Simple Simon to the pieman,
  "Indeed, I have not any."

Simple Simon went a-fishing
  For to catch a whale;
All the water he could find
  Was in his mother's pail.

Simon went to catch a bird,
  And thought he could not fail,
Because he had a pinch of salt
  To put upon his tail.

I KNOW A MAN

I know a man named Michael Finnegan—
He wears whiskers on his chinnegan.
Along came a wind and blew them in again;
Poor old Michael Finnegan,
                                    begin again

BARBER, BARBER

Barber, barber, shave a pig;
How many hairs will make a wig?
"Four-and-twenty, that's enough."
Give the poor barber a pinch of snuff.

THERE WAS A CROOKED MAN

There was a crooked man,
And he went a crooked mile,
He found a crooked sixpence,
Against a crooked stile;
He bought a crooked cat
Which caught a crooked mouse,
And they all lived together
In a little crooked house.

JACK SPRAT

Jack Sprat could eat no fat.
His wife could eat no lean;
And so betwixt the two of them,
They licked the platter clean.

OLD KING COLE

Old King Cole
Was a merry old soul,
And a merry old soul was he;
He called for his pipe,
He called for his bowl,
And he called for his fiddlers three.

Every fiddler, he had a fine fiddle
And a very fine fiddle had he;
Then twee, tweedle-dee,
Tweedle-dee went the fiddlers.
Oh, there's none so rare
As can compare
With King Cole and his fiddlers three!

THE
QUEEN
OF
HEARTS

The Queen of Hearts,
She made some tarts,
All on a summer's day.

The Knave of Hearts,
He stole those tarts,
And took them clean away.

The King of Hearts
Called for the tarts,
And beat the Knave full sore.

The Knave of Hearts
Brought back the tarts,
And vowed he'd steal no more.

TOMMY TUCKER

Little Tommy Tucker
Sings for his supper.
What shall he eat?
White bread and butter.

How shall he cut it
Without any knife?
How shall he marry
Without any wife?

HOT CROSS BUNS

Hot cross buns!
Hot cross buns!
One a penny, two a penny,
Hot cross buns!
If you have no daughters,
Give them to your sons.
One a penny, two a penny,
Hot cross buns!

POLLY,
PUT THE
KETTLE ON

Polly, put the kettle on,
Polly, put the kettle on,
Polly, put the kettle on,
We'll all have tea!

Sukey, take it off again,
Sukey, take it off again,
Sukey, take it off again,
They're all gone away.

SING A SONG
OF SIXPENCE

Sing a song of sixpence,
    A pocket full of rye,
Four and twenty blackbirds
    Baked in a pie.
When the pie was opened,
    The birds began to sing.
Wasn't that a dainty dish
    To set before the King?

The King was in his counting house
    Counting out his money;
The Queen was in her parlor,
    Eating bread and honey;
The maid was in the garden,
    Hanging out the clothes,
Down came a blackbird
    And snapped off her nose.
But there came a Jenny Wren
    And popped it on again.

Old Mother Hubbard

Old Mother Hubbard
Went to the cupboard,
To get her poor dog a bone;
But when she got there,
The cupboard was bare,
And so the poor dog had none.

She went to the baker's
To buy him some bread,
But when she came back,
The poor dog was dead.

She went to the fruiterer's
To buy him some fruit,
But when she came back,
He was playing the flute.

She went to the fishmonger's
To buy him some fish,
But when she came back,
He was licking the dish.

She went to the barber's
To buy him a wig,
But when she came back,
He was dancing a jig.

She went to the cobbler's
To buy him some shoes,
But when she came back,
He was reading the news.

She went to the tailor's
To buy him a coat,
But when she came back,
He was riding a goat.

The dame made a curtsy,
The dog made a bow;
The dame said, "Your servant,"
The dog said, "Bow-wow."

WIND IN THE EAST

When the wind is in the East,
'Tis neither good for man nor beast;
When the wind is in the North,
The skillful fisher goes not forth;
When the wind is in the South,
It blows the bait in the fishes' mouth;
When the wind is in the West,
Then 'tis at the very best.

DOCTOR FOSTER

Doctor Foster went to Gloucester,
In a shower of rain.
He stepped in a puddle,
Up to the middle,
And never went there again.

A SUNSHINY SHOWER

A sunshiny shower
  Won't last an hour.

MARCH WINDS

March winds and April showers
Bring forth May flowers.

ONE MISTY, MOISTY MORNING

One misty, moisty morning,
When cloudy was the weather,
There I met an old man
Clothed all in leather.
He began to compliment
And I began to grin,
"How-do-you-do,"
And "how-do-you-do,"
And "how-do-you-do, again!"

THE
NORTH
WIND
DOTH
BLOW

The north wind doth blow,
  And we shall have snow,
And what will poor Robin do then, poor thing?
  He'll sit in a barn,
  To keep himself warm,
And hide his head under his wing, poor thing.

WEE WILLIE WINKIE

Wee Willie Winkie
  Runs through the town,
Upstairs and downstairs
  In his nightgown,
Rapping at the window,
  Crying through the lock,
"Are the children in their beds?
  For now it's eight o'clock."

IT'S RAINING, IT'S POURING

It's raining, it's pouring,
The old man's a-snoring.
He went to bed
And bumped his head
And couldn't get up in the morning.

JEREMIAH OBEDIAH

Jeremiah Obediah puffs, puffs, puffs,
When he gets his messages he snuffs, snuffs, snuffs,
When he goes to school by day he roars, roars, roars,
And when he goes to bed at night he snores, snores, snores.

DIDDLE, DIDDLE, DUMPLING

Diddle, diddle, dumpling, my son John,
He went to bed with his stockings on;
One shoe off, and one shoe on,
Diddle, diddle, dumpling, my son John.

GOOD NIGHT

The rabbits play no more,
   The little birds are weary,
The buttercups are folded up—
   Good night, good night, my dearie.

The children in the country,
   The children in the city
Go to their beds with nodding heads—
   Good night, good night, my pretty.

ROSE FYLEMAN

DOWN WITH
THE LAMBS

Down with the lambs,
   Up with the lark,
Run to bed, children,
   Before it gets dark.

Poems for outdoors

LITTLE SEEDS
WE SOW IN SPRING

Little seeds we sow in spring
growing while the robins sing,
give us carrots, peas and beans,
tomatoes, pumpkins, squash and greens.

And we pick them,
one and all,
through the summer,
through the fall.

Winter comes, then spring, and then
little seeds we sow again.

ELSE HOLMELUND MINARIK

SPRING

as my eyes
search
the prairie
I feel the summer
in the spring

CHIPPEWA INDIAN POEM

54

SPRING WIND

The west wind dances down the lane
  and sets the robins winging;
It has a message sweet and plain,
  for some folks hear it singing:
O hurry, gather daffodils! They're scattered over all the hills
  As thick as anything!
The little buds unfold again, in buff and white and gold again—
  It's Spring, Spring, Spring!

The west wind races up the road
  and sets the green grass sprouting;
It wakes the turtle and the toad,
  and some folks hear it shouting:
O hurry, fetch your bat and ball, put on your oldest shoes of all,
  And cap and everything.
It's turning fine and hot again, the boys are in the lot again—
  It's Spring, Spring, Spring!

NANCY BYRD TURNER

55

SPRING MORNING

Where am I going? I don't quite know.
Down to the stream where the king-cups grow—
Up on the hill where the pine trees blow—
Anywhere, anywhere. *I* don't know.

Where am I going? The clouds sail by,
Little ones, baby ones, over the sky.
Where am I going? The shadows pass,
Little ones, baby ones, over the grass.

If you were a cloud, and sailed up there,
You'd sail on water as blue as air,
And you'd see me here in the fields and say:
"Doesn't the sky look green today?"

Where am I going? The high rooks call:
"It's awful fun to be born at all."
Where am I going? The ring-doves coo:
"We do have beautiful things to do."

If you were a bird, and lived on high,
You'd lean on the wind when the wind came by,
You'd say to the wind when it took you away:
"*That's* where I wanted to go today!"

Where am I going? I don't quite know.
What does it matter where people go?
Down to the wood where the bluebells grow—
Anywhere, anywhere, *I* don't know.

A. A. MILNE

THE YEAR'S AT THE SPRING

The year's at the spring
And day's at the morn;
Morning's at seven;
The hillside's dew-pearled;
The lark's on the wing;
The snail's on the thorn:
God's in His heaven—
All's right with the world!

ROBERT BROWNING

BAREFOOT DAYS

In the morning, very early,
That's the time I love to go
Barefoot where the fern grows curly
And grass is cool between each toe,
On a summer morning—O!
On a summer morning!

That is when the birds go by
Up the sunny slopes of air,
And each rose has a butterfly
Or a golden bee to wear;
And I am glad in every toe—
Such a summer morning—O!
Such a summer morning!

RACHEL FIELD

A SUMMER MORNING

I saw dawn creep across the sky,
And all the gulls go flying by.
I saw the sea put on its dress
Of blue midsummer loveliness,
And heard the trees begin to stir
Green arms of pine and juniper.
I heard the wind call out and say:
"Get up, my dear, it is today!"

RACHEL FIELD

SUMMER EVENING

The sandy cat by the Farmer's chair
Mews at his knee for dainty fare;
Old Rover in his moss-greened house
Mumbles a bone, and barks at a mouse.
In the dewy fields the cattle lie
Chewing the cud 'neath a fading sky;
Dobbin at manger pulls his hay:
Gone is another summer's day.

WALTER DE LA MARE

BED IN SUMMER

In winter I get up at night
And dress by yellow candlelight.
In summer, quite the other way,
I have to go to bed by day.

I have to go to bed and see
The birds still hopping on the tree,
Or hear the grown-up people's feet
Still going past me in the street.

And does it not seem hard to you,
When all the sky is clear and blue,
And I should like so much to play,
To have to go to bed by day?

ROBERT LOUIS STEVENSON

AUTUMN FIRES

In the other gardens
  And all up the vale,
From the autumn bonfires
  See the smoke trail!

Pleasant summer over
  And all the summer flowers
The red fire blazes,
  The gray smoke towers.

Sing a song of seasons!
  Something bright in all!
Flowers in the summer,
  Fires in the fall!

                    ROBERT LOUIS STEVENSON

AUTUMN

The morns are meeker than they were,
  The nuts are getting brown;
The berry's cheek is plumper,
  The rose is out of town.
The maple wears a gayer scarf,
  The field a scarlet gown.
Lest I should be old-fashioned,
  I'll put a trinket on.

                    EMILY DICKINSON

A
VAGABOND
SONG

There is something in the autumn
        that is native to my blood—
Touch of manner, hint of mood;
And my heart is like a rhyme,
With the yellow and the purple
        and the crimson keeping time.

The scarlet of the maples
        can shake me like a cry
Of bugles going by.
And my lonely spirit thrills
To see the frosty asters
        like a smoke upon the hills.

There is something in October
        sets the gypsy blood astir;
We must rise and follow her,
When from every hill of flame
She calls and calls each vagabond by name.

BLISS CARMAN

THE MIST AND ALL

I like the fall,
The mist and all.
I like the night owl's
Lonely call—
And wailing sound
Of wind around.

I like the gray
November day,
And bare dead boughs
That coldly sway
Against my pane.
I like the rain.

I like to sit
And laugh at it—
And tend
My cozy fire a bit.
I like the fall—
The mist and all.

DIXIE WILLSON

AUTUMN SONG

These are the days of falling leaves,
The days of hazy weather,
Smelling of gold chrysanthemums
And gray wood smoke together.

These are the nights of nearby stars,
The nights of closer moons,
When the windy darkness echoes
To crickets' farewell tunes.

ELIZABETH-ELLEN LONG

WINTER

The street cars are
Like frosted cakes—
All covered up
With cold snowflakes.

The horses' hoofs
Scrunch on the street;
Their eyelashes
Are white with sleet.

And everywhere
The people go
With faces *tickled*
By the snow.

DOROTHY ALDIS

THE SNOWBIRD

When all the ground with snow is white,
     The merry snowbird comes,
And hops about with great delight
     To find the scattered crumbs.

How glad he seems to get to eat
     A piece of cake or bread!
He wears no shoes upon his feet,
     Nor hat upon his head.

But happiest is he, I know,
     Because no cage with bars
Keeps him from walking on the snow
     And printing it with stars.

FRANK DEMPSTER SHERMAN

March

June

September

December

THE MONTHS

January brings the snow,
Makes our feet and fingers glow.

February brings the rain,
Thaws the frozen lake again.

March brings breezes, loud and shrill,
To stir the dancing daffodil.

April brings the primrose sweet,
Scatters daisies at our feet.

May brings flocks of pretty lambs
Skipping by their fleecy dams.

June brings tulips, lilies, roses,
Fills the children's hands with posies.

Hot July brings cooling showers,
Apricots, and gillyflowers.

August brings the sheaves of corn;
Then the harvest home is borne.

Warm September brings the fruit;
Sportsmen then begin to shoot.

Fresh October brings the pheasant;
Then to gather nuts is pleasant.

Dull November brings the blast;
Then the leaves are whirling fast.

Chill December brings the sleet,
Blazing fire, and Christmas treat.

SARA COLERIDGE

JANUARY

January opens
The box of the year
And brings out days
That are bright and clear.
And brings out days
That are cold and gray,
And shouts, "Come see
What I brought today!"

LELAND B. JACOBS

FEBRUARY
TWILIGHT

I stood beside a hill
    Smooth with new-laid snow,
A single star looked out
    From the cold evening glow.

There was no other creature
    That saw what I could see—
I stood and watched the evening star
    As long as it watched me.

SARA TEASDALE

MARCH

Dear March, come in!
How glad I am!
I looked for you before.
Put down your hat—
You must have walked—
How out of breath you are!
Dear March, how are you?
And the rest?
Did you leave Nature well?
Oh, March,
    come right upstairs with me,
I have so much to tell!

EMILY DICKINSON

APRIL

The roofs are shining from the rain,
    The sparrows twitter as they fly,
And with a windy April grace
    The little clouds go by.

Yet the back yards are bare and brown
    With only one unchanging tree—
I could not be so sure of Spring
    Save that it sings in me.

SARA TEASDALE

MAY MORNINGS

May mornings are merry,
May mornings are gay,
For every green hedgerow
Is fragrant with may,
And every blithe blackbird
Is singing like mad,
And nothing is dreary
Or weary or sad.
The sun's warm and friendly,
The breeze soft and cool,
And gay little children
Go dancing to school.

IVY O. EASTWICK

Robert McCloskey

STAY, JUNE, STAY!

The days are clear
   Day after day,
When April's here
   That leads to May,
And June
Must follow soon:
   Stay, June, stay!—
If only we could stop the moon
And June!

CHRISTINA ROSSETTI

JULY

When the scarlet cardinal tells
   Her dream to the dragonfly,
And the lazy breeze makes a nest in the trees,
   And murmurs a lullaby,
   It is July.

When the tangled cobweb pulls
   The cornflower's cap awry,
And the lilies tall lean over the wall
   To bow to the butterfly,
   It is July.

When the heat like a mist veil floats,
   And poppies flame in the rye,
And the silver note in the streamlet's throat
   Has softened almost to a sigh,
   It is July.

When the hours are so still that time
   Forgets them, and lets them lie
'Neath petals pink till the night stars wink
   At the sunset in the sky,
   It is July.

SUSAN HARTLEY SWETT

IN AUGUST

When the sun is strong
And the day is hot,
We move around
At a peaceful trot.
We don't wear much
In the way of clothes
And we squirt ourselves
With the garden hose.

MARCHETTE CHUTE

GLIMPSE IN AUTUMN

Ladies at a ball
    Are not so fine as these
Richly brocaded trees
    That decorate the fall.

They stand against a wall
    Of crisp October sky,
Their plumèd heads held high,
    Like ladies at a ball.

JEAN STARR UNTERMEYER

SEPTEMBER

A road like brown ribbon,
    A sky that is blue,
A forest of green
    With that sky peeping through.

Asters, deep purple,
    A grasshopper's call,
Today it is summer,
    Tomorrow is fall.

EDWINA FALLIS

OCTOBER

The summer is over,
    The trees are all bare,
There is mist in the garden
    And frost in the air.
The meadows are empty
    And gathered the sheaves—
But isn't it lovely
    Kicking up leaves!

John from the garden
    Has taken the chairs;
It's dark in the evening
    And cold on the stairs.
Winter is coming
    And everyone grieves—
But isn't it lovely
    Kicking up leaves!

ROSE FYLEMAN

NOVEMBER

November comes,
And November goes
With the last red berries
And the first white snows,

With night coming early
And dawn coming late,
And ice in the bucket
And frost by the gate.

The fires burn
And the kettles sing,
And earth sinks to rest
Until next spring.

ELIZABETH COATSWORTH

DECEMBER

I like days
with a snow-white collar,
and nights when the moon
is a silver dollar,
and hills are filled
with eiderdown stuffing
and your breath makes smoke
like an engine puffing.

I like days
when feathers are snowing,
and all the eaves
have petticoats showing,
and the air is cold,
and the wires are humming,
but you feel all warm . . .
with Christmas coming!

AILEEN FISHER

AN OLD CHRISTMAS GREETING

Sing hey! Sing hey!
For Christmas Day;
Twine mistletoe and holly,
For friendship glows
In winter snows,
And so let's all be jolly.

AUTHOR UNKNOWN

CHECK

The Night was creeping on the ground!
She crept and did not make a sound,

Until she reached the tree: And then
She covered it, and stole again

Along the grass beside the wall!
—I heard the rustling of her shawl

As she threw blackness everywhere
Along the sky, the ground, the air,

And in the room where I was hid!
But, no matter what she did

To everything that was without,
She could not put my candle out!

So I stared at the Night! And she
Stared back solemnly at me!

JAMES STEPHENS

MOON SONG

There is a star that runs very fast,
That goes pulling the moon
Through the tops of the poplars.
It is all in silver,
The tall star:
The moon rolls goldenly along
Out of breath—
Mr. Moon, does he make you hurry?

HILDA CONKLING

THIS IS MY ROCK

This is my rock
And here I run
To steal the secret of the sun;

This is my rock
And here come I
Before the night has swept the sky;

This is my rock,
This is the place
I meet the evening face to face.

DAVID MCCORD

MOON-IN-WATER

Three Wise Men of Gotham
thought the Moon was cheese
and tried to fish it out
of the river—if you please!
but all the little tadpoles
trilled a little tune:
"You'll never, never catch it—
it's the Moon!
            Moon!
                    MOON!"

IVY O. EASTWICK

THE FALLING STAR

I saw a star slide down the sky,
Blinding the north as it went by,
Too burning and too quick to hold,
Too lovely to be bought or sold,
Good only to make wishes on
And then forever to be gone.

76   SARA TEASDALE

STARS

Bright stars, light stars,
Shining-in-the-night stars,
Little twinkly, winkly stars,
Deep in the sky!

Yellow stars, red stars,
Shine-when-I'm-in-bed stars,
Oh how many blinky stars,
Far, far away!

RHODA W. BACMEISTER

TWINKLE, TWINKLE, LITTLE STAR

Twinkle, twinkle, little star,
How I wonder what you are!
Up above the world so high,
Like a diamond in the sky.

JANE TAYLOR

NIGHT

My kitten walks on velvet feet
And makes no sound at all;
And in the doorway nightly sits
To watch the darkness fall.

I think he loves the lady, Night,
And feels akin to her
Whose footsteps are as still as his,
Whose touch as soft as fur.

LOIS WEAKLEY McKAY

SUNRISE

I've never seen the great sun rise,
For then I am in bed;
The sands of slumber in my eyes
Hold down my drowsy head.

I *think* the sun climbs up the sky
And throws the clouds away,
Then girds her flaming tunic high
And strides to meet the day.

Soft-touched by birds' wings is her head;
Her feet caressed by trees;
She turns their leaves to gold and red
And stoops to drink the seas.

KATHARINE KOSMAK

THE SUN

I told the Sun that I was glad,
I'm sure I don't know why;
Somehow the pleasant way he had
Of shining in the sky
Just put a notion in my head
That wouldn't it be fun
If, walking on the hill, I said
"I'm happy" to the Sun.

JOHN DRINKWATER

SONG OF THE
WAKE-UP-WORLD

Wake up, O World; O World, awake!
The light is bright on hill and lake;
O World, awake; wake up, O World!
The flags of the wind are all unfurled;
Wake up, O World; O World, awake!
Of earth's delightfulness partake.

Wake up, O World, whatever hour;
Sweet are the fields, sweet is the flower!
Wake up, O World; O World, awake;
Perhaps to see the daylight break,
Perhaps to see the sun descend,
The night begin, the daylight end.

But something surely to behold,
Not bought with silver or with gold,
Not shown in any land of dreams.
For open eyes the whole world teems
With lovely things to do or make,
Wake up, O World; O World, awake!

COUNTEE CULLEN

MORNING

Will there really be a morning?
    Is there such a thing as day?
Could I see it from the mountains
    If I were as tall as they?
Has it feet like water lilies?
    Has it feathers like a bird?
Is it brought from famous countries
    Of which I've never heard?
Oh, some scholar! Oh, some sailor!
    Oh, some wise man from the skies!
Please to tell a little pilgrim
    Where the place called *morning* lies!

EMILY DICKINSON

AFTERNOON ON A HILL

I will be the gladdest thing
    Under the sun!
I will touch a hundred flowers
    And not pick one.

I will look at cliffs and clouds
    With quiet eyes,
Watch the wind bow down the grass,
    And the grass rise.

And when lights begin to show
    Up from the town,
I will mark which must be mine,
    And then start down!

EDNA ST. VINCENT MILLAY

MY SHADOW

I have a little shadow that goes in and out with me,
And what can be the use of him is more than I can see.
He is very, very like me from the heels up to the head;
And I see him jump before me, when I jump into my bed.

The funniest thing about him is the way he likes to grow—
Not at all like proper children, which is always very slow;
For he sometimes shoots up taller like an India-rubber ball,
And he sometimes gets so little that there's none of him at all.

He hasn't got a notion of how children ought to play,
And can only make a fool of me in every sort of way.
He stays so close beside me, he's a coward you can see;
I'd think shame to stick to nursie as that shadow sticks to me!

One morning, very early, before the sun was up,
I rose and found the shining dew on every buttercup;
But my lazy little shadow, like an arrant sleepyhead,
Had stayed at home behind me and was fast asleep in bed.

ROBERT LOUIS STEVENSON

SHADOW
DANCE

O Shadow,
Dear Shadow,
Come, Shadow,
And dance!
On the wall
In the firelight
Let both of
Us prance!
I raise my
Arms, thus!
And you raise
Your arms, so!
And dancing
And leaping
And laughing
We go!
From the wall
To the ceiling,
From ceiling
To wall,
Just you and
I, Shadow,
And none else
At all.

IVY O. EASTWICK

THE WIND

I saw you toss the kites on high
And blow the birds about the sky;
And all around I heard you pass,
Like ladies' skirts across the grass—
    O wind, a-blowing all day long,
    O wind, that sings so loud a song!

I saw the different things you did,
But always you yourself you hid.
I felt you push, I heard you call,
I could not see yourself at all—
    O wind, a-blowing all day long,
    O wind, that sings so loud a song!

O you that are so strong and cold,
O blower, are you young or old?
Are you a beast of field and tree,
Or just a stronger child than me?
    O wind, a-blowing all day long,
    O wind, that sings so loud a song!

ROBERT LOUIS STEVENSON

WHO HAS SEEN THE WIND?

Who has seen the wind?
  Neither I nor you;
But when the leaves hang trembling,
  The wind is passing through.

Who has seen the wind?
  Neither you nor I;
But when the trees
  Bow down their heads,
The wind is passing by.

CHRISTINA ROSSETTI

WIND CAPERS

The wind is out with a leap and a twirl,
   Prancing, prancing,
The aspen tree is like a girl,
   Dancing, dancing.
The maple tree upon the hill,
   She cannot keep her ruffles still.
The swallows blow along the sky,
   Glancing, glancing,
O wind, O wind, you tricky elf,
   Behave yourself!

NANCY BYRD TURNER

CLOUDS

White sheep, white sheep,
On a blue hill,
When the wind stops
You all stand still.
When the wind blows
You walk away slow.
White sheep, white sheep,
Where do you go?

CHRISTINA ROSSETTI

BROOMS

On stormy days
When the wind is high
Tall trees are brooms
Sweeping the sky.

They swish their branches
In buckets of rain,
And swash and sweep it
Blue again.

DOROTHY ALDIS

GARMENT

The clouds weave a shawl
Of downy plaid
For the sky to put on
When the weather's bad.

LANGSTON HUGHES

FROM THE SKY

All sorts
of things
come down from
the sky—
snowflakes like
goose-feathers
flutter
and fly;
wild winds like
grey gulls go
whirling
around;
moonbeams like
fireflies dance
over
the ground;
raindrops like
jewels fall
down on
the meadows;
and last come
the shadows—
shadows—
like shadows.

IVY O. EASTWICK

89

IN TIME OF SILVER RAIN

In time of silver rain
The butterflies lift silken wings
To catch a rainbow cry,
And trees put forth
New leaves to sing
In joy beneath the sky
As down the roadway passing boys
And girls go singing, too,
In time of silver rain
When spring
And life are new.

LANGSTON HUGHES

RAIN, RAIN, GO AWAY

Rain, rain, go away,
Come again another day;
Little Johnny wants to play.

OLD RHYME

DOWN THE RAIN FALLS

Down the rain falls,
Up crackles the fire,
Tick-tock goes the clock
Neither lower nor higher—

Such soft little sounds
As sleepy hens make
When they talk to themselves
For company's sake.

ELIZABETH COATSWORTH

RAIN

The rain is raining all around,
It falls on field and tree,
It rains on the umbrellas here,
And on the ships at sea.

ROBERT LOUIS STEVENSON

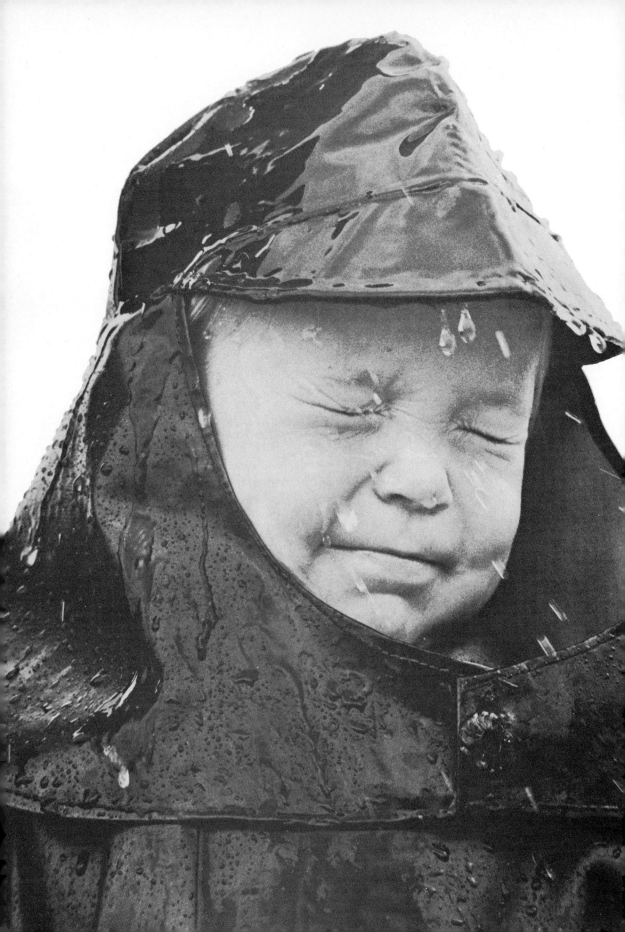

THE UMBRELLA BRIGADE

"Pitter patter!" falls the rain
On the schoolroom windowpane.
Such a plashing! such a dashing!
Will it e'er be dry again?
Down the gutter rolls a flood,
And the crossing's deep in mud;
And the puddles! oh, the puddles
Are a sight to stir one's blood!

Chorus.
But let it rain
Tree toads and frogs,
Muskets and pitchforks,
Kittens and dogs!
Dash away! plash away!
Who is afraid?
Here we go,
The Umbrella Brigade!

Pull the boots up to the knee!
Tie the hoods on merrily!
Such a hustling! such a jostling!
Out of breath with fun are we.
Clatter, clatter, down the street,
Greeting every one we meet,
With our laughing and our chaffing,
Which the laughing drops repeat.

Chorus.
So let it rain
Tree toads and frogs,
Muskets and pitchforks,
Kittens and dogs
Dash away! plash away!
Who is afraid?
Here we go,
The Umbrella Brigade!

LAURA E. RICHARDS

RAIN IN THE NIGHT

Raining, raining,
All night long;
Sometimes loud, sometimes soft,
Just like a song.

There'll be rivers in the gutters
And lakes along the street.
It will make our lazy kitty
Wash his little dirty feet.

The roses will wear diamonds
Like kings and queens at court;
But the pansies all get muddy
Because they are so short.

I'll sail my boat tomorrow
In wonderful new places,
But first I'll take my watering pot
And wash the pansies' faces.

AMELIA JOSEPHINE BURR

SINGING

Of speckled eggs the birdie sings
    And nests among the trees;
The sailor sings of ropes and things
    In ships upon the seas.

The children sing in far Japan,
    The children sing in Spain;
The organ with the organ man
    Is singing in the rain.

ROBERT LOUIS STEVENSON

DRUMS OF THE RAIN

The drum is our big windowpane!
The drumsticks are the drops of rain!
"Rat-a-tat-tat! Rat-a-tat-tat!
Boom! Boom! Boom!"
The drums, the drums are beating,
And filling all the room!
"Boom, boom, boom!
  Rat-a-tat-tat! Rat-a-tat-tat!
Boom!"
The snare drums are the raindrops
That rattle in the room;
The thunder is the big, round drum
That says, "Boom! Boom!"
We're happy when a rain storm comes,
Because it brings the drums, THE DRUMS!

MARY CAROLYN DAVIES

JACKY FROST

Jacky Frost, Jacky Frost,
 Came in the night;
Left the meadows that he crossed
 All gleaming white.
Painted with his silver brush
 Every windowpane;
Kissed the leaves and made them blush,
 Blush and blush again.

Jacky Frost, Jacky Frost,
 Crept around the house,
Sly as a silver fox,
 Still as a mouse.
Out little Jenny came,
 Blushing like a rose;
Up jumped Jacky Frost,
 And pinched her little nose.

LAURA E. RICHARDS

LOOK AT THE SNOW!

Look at the snow!
 Look at the snow!
Let's all take our sleds,
 And go!
Up the hill we walk slow, slow,
And drag our red sleds in the snow;
But once at the top of the hill, we know
That like the wind they'll go, go, go,
Whizzing down to the flat, below.
Oh, the fun as we swiftly fly
Over the snow like a bird on high!
It takes our breath as our sleds speed by;
No one's as happy as you and I!
—Summers may come, and summers may go,
But *we* like the snow, the snow, the snow!

MARY CAROLYN DAVIES

SLIDING

We can slide
       down
            the
                 hill
    or
       down
           the
              stair
    or
       down
           the
              street
    or anywhere.
Or down the roof
    where the shingles broke,
Or down the trunk
    of the back-yard oak.

Down
   the
     slide
       or the ice
       or the slippery street,

We can slide on our sled
    on our skates
    on our feet.
Oh, it's lots of fun to go outside
    And slide
       and slide
          and slide
             and slide.

MYRA COHN LIVINGSTON

SLEET STORM

TIC-TIC-TIC!
The sound of the sleet
Fell like the beat
Of tiny feet,
Racing and chasing down the street:
The quick sharp beat
Of a million hoofs
Clicked and clattered
Across the roofs.
The sleet storm fell
Through a day and a night
With a tic-tic-tic
That was fast and light.

On the second morning
A cold sun shone
On a glittering, crystal,
Frigid zone.
Each bush and branch
Was icily hung
With the frozen song
The sleet had sung.
The branches swayed
With their icy load
Where millions of diamonds
Flashed and glowed.
Steep roofs shone
With a blinding glare,
Fringed with icicles
Everywhere.
But the tic-tic-tic
Of the sleet was still,
Caught on each glistening
Valley and hill.

JAMES S. TIPPETT

ICE

When it is the winter time
   I run up the street
And I make the ice laugh
   With my little feet—
"Crickle, crackle, crickle
   Crrreeet, crrreeet, crrreeet."

DOROTHY ALDIS

THAW

The snow is soft,
   and how it squashes!
"Galumph, galumph!"
   go my galoshes.

EUNICE TIETJENS

FOG

The fog comes
on little cat feet.
It sits looking
over harbor and city
on silent haunches
and then moves on.

CARL SANDBURG

poems
about
plants
and
Animals

VOL I

LIVING
ANIMALS
OF THE
WORLD

A KITTEN

He's nothing much but fur
And two round eyes of blue,
He has a giant purr
And a midget mew.

He darts and pats the air,
He starts and cocks his ear,
When there is nothing there
For him to see and hear.

He runs around in rings,
But why we cannot tell;
With sideways leaps he springs
At things invisible—

Then halfway through a leap
His startled eyeballs close,
And he drops off to sleep
With one paw on his nose.

ELEANOR FARJEON

LITTLE PUSSY

I like little Pussy,
Her coat is so warm;
And if I don't hurt her,
She'll do me no harm.

So I'll not pull her tail,
Nor drive her away,
But Pussy and I
Very gently will play.

JANE TAYLOR

DOGS AND WEATHER

I'd like a different dog
    For every kind of weather—
A narrow greyhound for a fog,
    A wolfhound strange and white,
With a tail like a silver feather
    To run with in the night,
When snow is still, and winter stars are bright.

In the fall I'd like to see
    In answer to my whistle,
A golden spaniel look at me.
    But best of all for rain
A terrier, hairy as a thistle,
    To trot with fine disdain
Beside me down the soaked, sweet-smelling lane.

WINIFRED WELLES

DOGS

The dogs I know
Have many shapes.
For some are big and tall,
And some are long,
And some are thin,
And some are fat and small.
And some are little bits of fluff
And have no shape at all.

MARCHETTE CHUTE

HOLDING HANDS

Elephants walking
Along the trails

Are holding hands
By holding tails.

Trunks and tails
Are handy things

When elephants walk
In circus rings.

Elephants work
And elephants play

And elephants walk
And feel so gay.

And when they walk—
It never fails

They're holding hands
By holding tails.

LENORE M. LINK

THE ELEPHANT

When people call this beast to mind,
They marvel more and more
At such a *little* tail behind,
So LARGE a trunk before.

HILAIRE BELLOC

WHISKY FRISKY

WHISKY Frisky,
Hippity-hop
Up he goes
To the treetop!

Whirly, twirly,
Round and round,
Down he scampers
To the ground.

Furly, curly,
What a tail!
Tall as a feather,
Broad as a sail!

Where's his supper?
In the shell,
Snap, cracky,
Out it fell.

AUTHOR UNKNOWN

THE REASON

Rabbits and squirrels
Are furry and fat,
And all of the chickens
Have feathers, and *that*
Is why when it's raining
They need not stay in
The way children do who have
Only their skin.

DOROTHY ALDIS

THE RABBIT

When they said the time to hide was mine,
I hid back under a thick grapevine.

And while I was still for the time to pass,
A little gray thing came out of the grass.

He hopped his way through the melon bed
And sat down close by a cabbage head.

He sat down close where I could see,
And his big still eyes looked hard at me,

His big eyes bursting out of the rim,
And I looked back very hard at him.

ELIZABETH MADOX ROBERTS

FURRY BEAR

If I were a bear,
  And a big bear too,
I shouldn't much care
  If it froze or snew;
I shouldn't much mind
  If it snowed or friz—
I'd be all fur-lined
  With a coat like his!

For I'd have fur boots and a brown fur wrap,
And brown fur knickers and a big fur cap.
I'd have a fur muffle-ruff to cover my jaws,
And brown fur mittens on my big brown paws.
With a big brown furry-down up to my head,
I'd sleep all the winter in a big fur bed.

A. A. MILNE

BABY GOAT

Did you ever pat a baby goat
And learn how soft he feels?
Did you ever watch him walk about
On his four little black high heels?

ZHENYA GAY

It is a curious thing that you
        don't wish to be a kangaroo,
                to hop hop hop
                        and never stop
        the whole day long and the whole night, too!

                to hop across Australian plains
                        with tails that sweep behind like trains
THE KANGAROO
                                and small front paws
                                and pointed jaws
                        and pale neat coats to shed the rains.

If skies be blue, if skies be gray,
        they bound in the same graceful way
                into dim space
                        at such a pace
        that where they go there's none to say!

ELIZABETH COATSWORTH

BIGGER

The cow is big. Her eyes are round.
She makes a very scary sound.

I'm rather glad the fence is tall—
I don't feel quite so weak and small.

And yet I'm not afraid. You see,
I'm six years old—and she's just three.

DOROTHY BROWN THOMPSON

THE COW

The friendly cow all red and white,
I love with all my heart:
She gives me cream with all her might,
To eat with apple tart.

She wanders lowing here and there,
And yet she cannot stray,
All in the pleasant open air,
The pleasant light of day;

And blown by all the winds that pass
And wet with all the showers,
She walks among the meadow grass
And eats the meadow flowers.

ROBERT LOUIS STEVENSON

HORSES

Back and forth
and up and down,
horses' tails go switching.

Up and down
and back and forth,
horses' skins go twitching.

Horses do
a lot of work
to keep themselves from itching.

AILEEN FISHER

jump or jiggle

Frogs jump
Caterpillars hump

Worms wiggle
Bugs jiggle

Rabbits hop
Horses clop

Snakes slide
Sea gulls glide

Mice creep
Deer leap

Puppies bounce
Kittens pounce

Lions stalk—
But—
I walk!

EVELYN BEYER

the little turtle

There was a little turtle.
He lived in a box.
He swam in a puddle.
He climbed on the rocks.

He snapped at a mosquito,
He snapped at a flea,
He snapped at a minnow.
And he snapped at me.

He caught the mosquito,
He caught the flea,
He caught the minnow.
But he didn't catch me.

VACHEL LINDSAY

snail

Little snail,
Dreaming you go.
Weather and rose
Is all you know.

Weather and rose
Is all you see,
Drinking
The dewdrop's
Mystery.

LANGSTON HUGHES

FUZZY WUZZY, CREEPY CRAWLY

Fuzzy wuzzy, creepy crawly
    Caterpillar funny,
You will be a butterfly
When the days are sunny.

Winging, flinging, dancing, springing
    Butterfly so yellow,
You were once a caterpillar,
    Wiggly, wiggly fellow.

LILLIAN SCHULZ

LITTLE BLACK BUG

Little black bug,
Little black bug,
Where have you been?
I've been under the rug,
Said little black bug.
Bug-ug-ug-ug.

Little green fly,
Little green fly,
Where have you been?
I've been way up high,
Said little green fly.
Bzzzzzzzzzzzzz.

Little old mouse,
Little old mouse,
Where have you been?
I've been all through the house,
Said little old mouse.
Squeak-eak-eak-eak-eak.

MARGARET WISE BROWN

AN EXPLANATION OF THE GRASSHOPPER

THE Grasshopper, the Grasshopper,
I will explain to you:—
He is the Brownies' racehorse,
The Fairies' Kangaroo.

VACHEL LINDSAY

THE CATERPILLAR

Brown and furry
Caterpillar in a hurry
Take your walk
To the shady leaf, or stalk,
Or what not,
Which may be the chosen spot.
No toad spy you,
Hovering bird of prey pass by you;
Spin and die,
To live again a butterfly.

CHRISTINA ROSSETTI

TO A FIREFLY

Stars are twinkling up on high,
Moon hangs low in eastern sky;
These with thee do not compare,
Cheerful beacon of the air—

Speeding onward through the dark,
Beneath the oak trees in the park,
With thy glowing, gleaming light,
Happy lightning bug of night.

J. MORRIS JONES

THE CRICKET

And when the rain had gone away
And it was shining everywhere,
I ran out on the walk to play
And found a little bug was there.

And he was running just as fast
As any little bug could run,
Until he stopped for breath at last,
All black and shiny in the sun.

And then he chirped a song to me
And gave his wings a little tug,
And *that's* the way he showed that he
Was very glad to be a bug!

MARJORIE BARROWS

FIREFLY (A *song*)

A little light is going by,
Is going up to see the sky,
A little light with wings.

I never could have thought of it,
To have a little bug all lit
And made to go on wings.

ELIZABETH MADOX ROBERTS

WHO IS SO PRETTY?

Skitter, skatter,
Leap and squeak!
We've been dancing
Half the week.

Under the sofa,
Along the shelf,
Every mouse
Is wild as an elf.

Big round ear
And bright black eye,
Nimble and natty,
Limber and spry—

Who is so pretty,
Who is so neat,
As a little mouse dancing
On little gray feet?

ELIZABETH COATSWORTH

MICE

I think mice
Are rather nice.

Their tails are long,
Their faces small,
They haven't any
Chins at all.
Their ears are pink,
Their teeth are white,
They run about
The house at night.
They nibble things
They shouldn't touch
And no one seems
To like them much.

But *I* think mice
Are nice.

118   ROSE FYLEMAN

THE HOUSE
OF THE MOUSE

The house of the mouse
is a wee little house,
a green little house in the grass,
which big clumsy folk
may hunt and may poke
and still never see as they pass
this sweet little, neat little,
wee little, green little,
cuddle-down hide-away
house in the grass.

LUCY SPRAGUE MITCHELL

THE CITY MOUSE
AND THE GARDEN MOUSE

The city mouse lives in a house;
The garden mouse lives in a bower,
He's friendly with the frogs and toads,
And sees the pretty plants in flower.

The city mouse eats bread and cheese;
The garden mouse eats what he can;
We will not grudge him seeds and stalks,
Poor little timid furry man.

CHRISTINA ROSSETTI

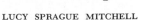

MOUSE

Little Mouse in gray velvet,
Have you had a cheese breakfast?
There are no crumbs on your coat,
Did you use a napkin?
I wonder what you had to eat,
And who dresses you in gray velvet?

HILDA CONKLING

SOMETHING TOLD THE WILD GEESE

Something told the wild geese
It was time to go.
Though the fields lay golden
Something whispered, "Snow."
Leaves were green and stirring,
Berries, luster-glossed,
But beneath warm feathers
Something cautioned, "Frost."
All the sagging orchards
Steamed with amber spice,
But each wild breast stiffened
At remembered ice.
Something told the wild geese
It was time to fly—
Summer sun was on their wings,
Winter in their cry.

RACHEL FIELD

THE WOODPECKER

The woodpecker pecked out a little round hole
And made him a house in the telephone pole.
One day when I watched he poked out his head,
And he had on a hood and a collar of red.

When the streams of rain pour out of the sky,
And the sparkles of lightning go flashing by,
And the big, big wheels of thunder roll,
He can snuggle back in the telephone pole.

120

ELIZABETH MADOX ROBERTS

SEA GULL

The sea gull curves his wings,
 the sea gull turns his eyes.
Get down into the water, fish!
 (if you are wise.)

The sea gull slants his wings,
 the sea gull turns his head.
Get deep into the water, fish!
 (or you'll be dead.)

ELIZABETH COATSWORTH

MRS. PECK-PIGEON

Mrs. Peck-Pigeon
Is picking for bread,
Bob—bob—bob
Goes her little round head.
Tame as a pussycat
In the street,
Step—step—step
Go her little red feet.
With her little red feet
And her little round head,
Mrs. Peck-Pigeon
Goes picking for bread.

ELEANOR FARJEON

TREES

Trees are the kindest things I know,

They do no harm, they simply grow

And spread a shade for sleepy cows,

And gather birds among their boughs.

They give us fruit in leaves above,

And wood to make our houses of,

And leaves to burn on Halloween,

And in the Spring new buds of green.

They are first when day's begun

To touch the beams of morning sun,

They are the last to hold the light

When evening changes into night,

And when a moon floats on the sky

They hum a drowsy lullaby

Of sleepy children long ago . . .

Trees are the kindest things I know.

HARRY BEHN

SONG

Elms are proud
and cedars dark,
poplars have silver
leaf-shadowed bark,
aspens whisper,
willows weep,
and all the tree toads
have gone to sleep.

ELIZABETH COATSWORTH

THE
BEECH
TREE

I'd like to have a garden
With a beech tree on the lawn;
The little birds that lived there
Would wake me up at dawn.

And in the summer weather
When all the leaves were green,
I'd sit beneath the beech boughs
And see the sky between.

ROSE FYLEMAN

QUEEN ANNE'S LACE

Queen Anne, Queen Anne, has washed her lace
  (She chose a summer's day)
And hung it in a grassy place
  To whiten, if it may.

Queen Anne, Queen Anne, has left it there,
  And slept the dewy night;
Then waked, to find the sunshine fair,
  And all the meadows white.

Queen Anne, Queen Anne, is dead and gone
  (She died a summer's day),
But left her lace to whiten on
  Each weed-entangled way!

MARY LESLIE NEWTON

124

NAMES

Larkspur and Hollyhock,
Pink Rose and purple Stock,
Lovely smelling Mignonette,
Lilies not quite opened yet,
Phlox the favorite of bees,
Bleeding Heart and Peonies—
Just their names are nice to say,
Softly,
On a summer's day.

DOROTHY ALDIS

DANDELIONS

Over the climbing meadows
Where the swallow shadows float,
These are the small gold buttons
On earth's green, windy coat.

FRANCES FROST

TOMMY

I put a seed into the ground
And said, "I'll watch it grow."
I watered it and cared for it
As well as I could know.

One day I walked in my back yard
And oh, what did I see!
My seed had popped itself right out,
Without consulting me.

GWENDOLYN BROOKS

CYCLE

So many little flowers
Drop their tiny heads
But newer buds come to bloom
In their place instead.

I miss the little flowers
That have gone away.
But the newly budding blossoms
Are equally gay.

LANGSTON HUGHES

Rhymes
of life
at home

SONG FOR A LITTLE HOUSE

I'm glad our house is a little house,
  Not too tall nor too wide:
I'm glad the hovering butterflies
  Feel free to come inside.

Our little house is a friendly house.
  It is not shy or vain;
It gossips with the talking trees,
  And makes friends with the rain.

And quick leaves cast a shimmer of green
  Against our whited walls,
And in the phlox the courteous bees
  Are paying duty calls.

CHRISTOPHER MORLEY

THE SHINY LITTLE HOUSE

I wish, how I wish, that I had a little house,
With a mat for the cat and a hole for the mouse,
And a clock going "tock" in a corner of the room
And a kettle, and a cupboard, and a big birch broom.

To school in the morning the children off would run,
And I'd give them a kiss and a penny and a bun.
But directly they had gone from this little house of mine,
I'd clap my hands and snatch a cloth,
  and shine, shine, shine.

I'd shine all the knives, all the windows and the floors,
All the grates, all the plates, all the handles on the doors,
Every fork, every spoon, every lid, and every tin,
Till everything was shining like a new bright pin.

At night, by the fire, when the children were in bed,
I'd sit and I'd knit, with a cap upon my head,
And the kettles and the saucepans,
  they would shine, shine, shine,
In this tweeny little, cosy little house of mine!

NANCY M. HAYES

MOVING

I like to move. There's such a feeling
Of hurrying
       and scurrying,
And such a feeling
Of men with trunks and packing cases,
Of kitchen clocks and mother's laces,
Dusters, dishes, books, and vases,
Toys and pans and candles.

I always find things I'd forgotten,
An old brown Teddy stuffed with cotton,
Some croquet mallets without handles,
A marble and my worn-out sandals,
A half an engine and a hat . . .
And I like that.

I like to watch the big vans backing,
And the lumbering
      and the cumbering,
And the hammering and the tacking.
I even like the packing!

And that will prove
I like to move!

EUNICE TIETJENS

THE NEW NEIGHBOR

Have you had your tonsils out?
  Do you go to school?
Do you know that there are frogs
  Down by the Willow Pool?

Are you good at cricket?
  Have you got a bat?
Do you know the proper way
  To feed a white rat?

Are there any apples
  On your apple tree?
Do you think your mother
  Will ask me in to tea?

ROSE FYLEMAN

A NEW FRIEND

They've taken in the furniture;
I watched them carefully.
I wondered, "Will there be a child
Just right to play with me?"

So I peeked through the garden fence
(I couldn't wait to see).
I found the little boy next door
Was peeking back at me.

MARJORIE ALLEN ANDERSON

SATURDAY SHOPPING

To market, to market,
On Saturday morn,
For prunes and potatoes
And ears of sweet corn,
For bacon and sausage,
For apple and pear.
To market, to market—
Our cupboard is bare!

KATHERINE EDELMAN

MIX A PANCAKE

Mix a pancake,
Stir a pancake,
        Pop it in the pan;

Fry the pancake,
Toss the pancake—
        Catch it if you can.

CHRISTINA ROSSETTI

SHELLING PEAS

I like to shell peas
that are fresh from a shop.
I start at the tail end
instead of the top
so they will explode
with a wonderful pop!

AILEEN FISHER

WHEN YOUNG MELISSA SWEEPS

When young Melissa sweeps a room
I vow she dances with the broom!

She curtsies in a corner brightly
And leads her partner forth politely.

Then up and down in jigs and reels,
With gold dust flying at their heels,

They caper. With a whirl or two
They make the wainscot shine like new;

They waltz beside the hearth, and quick
It brightens, shabby brick by brick.

A gay gavotte across the floor,
A Highland fling from door to door,

And every crack and corner's clean
Enough to suit a dainty queen.

If ever you are full of gloom,
Just watch Melissa sweep a room!

NANCY BYRD TURNER

FOOD

When I go walking down the street
There's lots of things I like to eat,

Like pretzels from the pretzel man
And buttered popcorn in a can,

And chocolate peppermints to lick
And candy apples on a stick.

Oh, there are many things to chew
While walking down the avenue.

MARCHETTE CHUTE

THE CUPBOARD

I know a little cupboard,
With a teeny tiny key,
And there's a jar of Lollipops
For me, me, me.

It has a little shelf, my dear,
As dark as dark can be,
And there's a dish of Banbury Cakes
For me, me, me.

I have a small fat grandmamma,
With a very slippery knee,
And she's Keeper of the Cupboard,
With the key, key, key.

And when I'm very good, my dear,
As good as good can be,
There's Banbury Cakes, and Lollipops
For me, me, me.

WALTER DE LA MARE

Animal Crackers

Animal crackers, and cocoa to drink,
That is the finest of suppers, I think;
When I'm grown up and can have what I please
I think I shall always insist upon these.

What do *you* choose when *you're* offered a treat?
When Mother says, "What would you like best to eat?"
Is it waffles and syrup, or cinnamon toast?
It's cocoa and animals that *I* love the most!

The kitchen's the coziest place that I know:
The kettle is singing, the stove is aglow,
And there in the twilight, how jolly to see
The cocoa and animals waiting for me.

Daddy and Mother dine later in state,
With Mary to cook for them, Susan to wait;
But they don't have nearly as much fun as I
Who eat in the kitchen with Nurse standing by;
And Daddy once said he would like to be me
Having cocoa and animals once more for tea!

CHRISTOPHER MORLEY

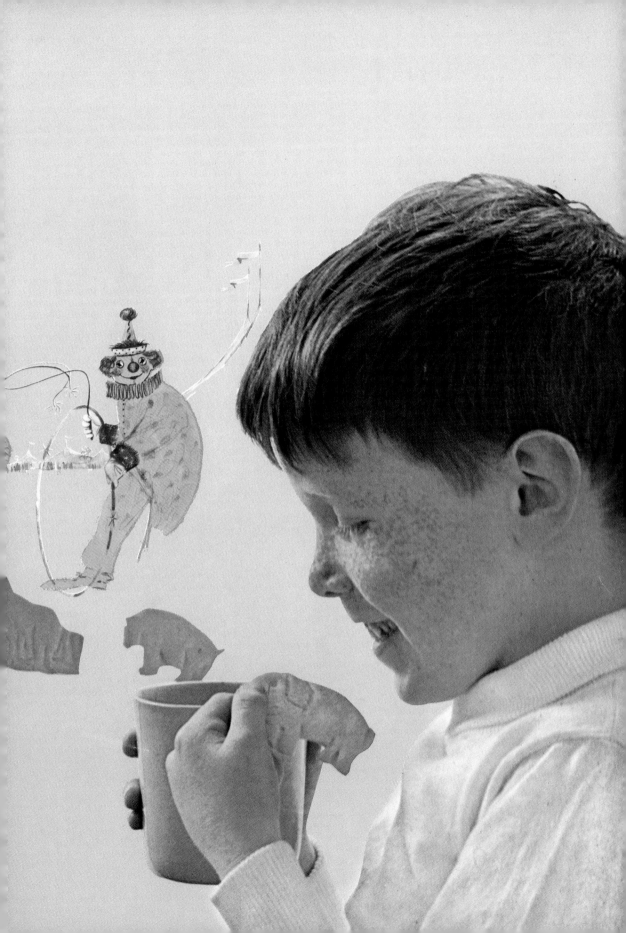

GALOSHES

Susie's galoshes
Make splishes and sploshes
And slooshes and sloshes,
As Susie steps slowly
Along in the slush.

They stamp and they tramp
On the ice and concrete,
They get stuck in the muck and the mud;
But Susie likes much best to hear

The slippery slush
As it slooshes and sloshes,
And splishes and sploshes,
All round her galoshes!

RHODA W. BACMEISTER

CHOOSING SHOES

New shoes, new shoes,
    Red and pink and blue shoes.
Tell me, what would *you* choose,
    If they'd let us buy?

Buckle shoes, bow shoes,
    Pretty pointy-toe shoes,
Strappy, cappy low shoes;
    Let's have some to try.

Bright shoes, white shoes,
    Dandy-dance-by-night shoes,
Perhaps-a-little-tight shoes,
    Like some? So would I.

    But

Flat shoes, fat shoes,
    Stump-along-like-that shoes,
Wipe-them-on-the-mat shoes,
    That's the sort they'll buy.

FFRIDA WOLFE

SHOES

My father has a pair of shoes
So beautiful to see!
I want to wear my father's shoes,
They are too big for me.

My baby brother has a pair,
As cunning as can be!
My feet won't go into that pair,
They are too small for me.

There's only one thing I can do
Till I get small or grown.
If I want to have a fitting shoe,
I'll have to wear my own.

TOM ROBINSON

THE MITTEN SONG

(*To be chanted*)

"Thumbs in the thumb-place,
Fingers all together!"
This is the song
We sing in mitten-weather.
When it is cold,
It doesn't matter whether
Mittens are wool,
Or made of finest leather.
This is the song
We sing in mitten-weather:
"Thumbs in the thumb-place,
Fingers all together!"

MARIE LOUISE ALLEN

MY ZIPPER SUIT

My zipper suit is bunny-brown—
The top zips up, the legs zip down.
I wear it every day.
My daddy brought it out from town.
Zip it up, and zip it down,
And hurry out to play!

MARIE LOUISE ALLEN

IN WINTER

When I have drunk my orange juice
And cocoa in a cup,
I put my woolly snowsuit on
And get it fastened up.

I go to school and take it off
And hang it on a rack.
And then when recess comes around
I have to hurry back.

And put it on to go and play,
And then when play is through
I take my snowsuit off again—
No easy thing to do.

And when it's time to leave for home
I heave a sigh, and then
I take that woolly suit of mine
And put it on again.

MARCHETTE CHUTE

ABOUT BUTTONS

Every button has a door
Which opens wide to let him in,
But when he rolls upon the floor,
Because he's tired of where he's been
And we can't find him any more,
We use a pin.

DOROTHY ALDIS

SINGING TIME

I wake in the morning early
And always, the very first thing,
I poke out my head and I sit up in bed
And I sing and I sing and I sing.

ROSE FYLEMAN

GROWING

I'm now tall enough
  To reach across the bed;
I put my toes on one side,
  On the other is my head.

L. J. STILES

TIME TO RISE

A birdie with a yellow bill
  Hopped upon the window sill,
Cocked his shining eye and said:
  "Ain't you 'shamed, you sleepyhead?"

ROBERT LOUIS STEVENSON

BREAKFAST TIME

The sun is always in the sky
Whenever I get out of bed,
And I often wonder why
It's never late.—My sister said

She didn't know who did the trick,
And that she didn't care a bit,
And I should eat my porridge quick,
. . . I think its mother wakens it.

JAMES STEPHENS   143

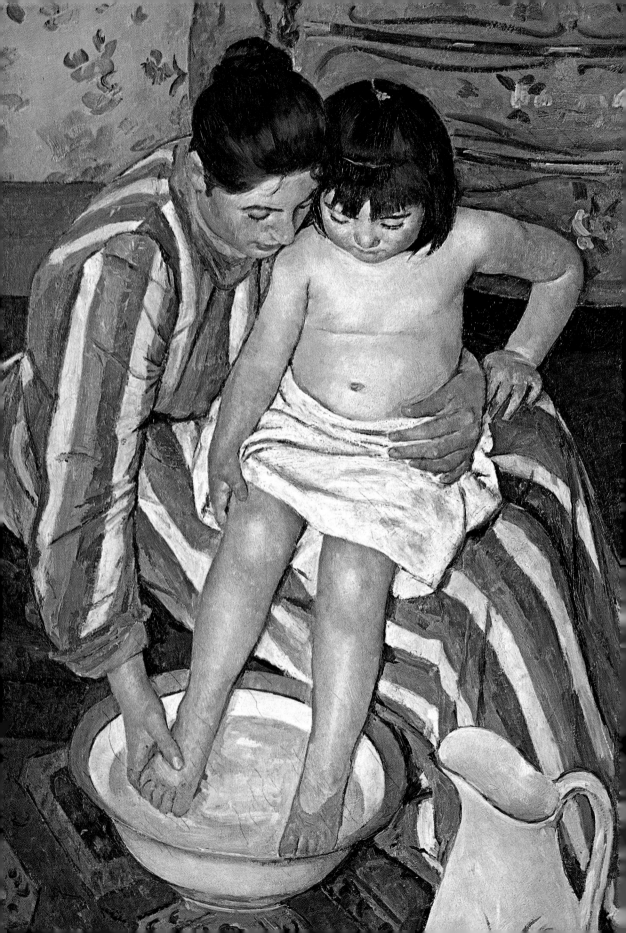

AN INDIGNANT MALE

The way they scrub
Me in the tub,
I think there's
      Hardly
      Any
      Doubt
Sometime they'll rub,
And rub and rub
Until they simply
      Rub
      Me
      Out.

ABRAM BUNN ROSS

AFTER A BATH

After my bath
I try, try, try
to wipe myself
till I'm dry, dry, dry.

Hands to wipe
and fingers and toes
and two wet legs
and a shiny nose.

Just think how much
less time I'd take
if I were a dog
and could shake, shake, shake.

AILEEN FISHER

NAUGHTY SOAP SONG

Just when I'm ready to
Start on my ears,
That is the time that my
Soap disappears.

It jumps from my fingers and
Slithers and slides
Down to the end of the
Tub, where it hides.

And acts in a most diso-
Bedient way
AND THAT'S WHY MY SOAP'S GROWING
THINNER EACH DAY.

DOROTHY ALDIS

145

WHEN I GET INTO BED

I'm never frightened in the dark,
Though I am very small;
I never sit all scared and hark
For Ogres in the hall.
But when my prayers are said
I have one awful dread,
That something waits to grab my toes
When I get into bed!

I try to think of pleasant things
Each time I get undressed;
And how each day no evil brings
If children do their best.
But the thought comes in my head,
As I'm turning down the spread,
That *something's* going to grab my toes
As I get into bed.

And when there's nothing more to do,
With bedclothes open wide,
It makes me shiver through and through
A-trying to decide
Which foot shall go ahead,
'Cause I'm sure I'd tumble dead
If something ever grabbed my toes
As I get into bed.

BURGES JOHNSON

THE SONG OF THE FROG

So hushaby, baby, if you'll go to sleep,
I'll give you a pretty red flower to keep.

But if you keep crying, a big ugly frog
Will croak by your side—kerchog! kerchog!

A DREAM PARTY

Lullaby, lullaby, slumberland bound,
When our baby's sleeping sound,
We'll go out and buy a fish
And call our friends to share the dish.
And when they ask what feast we're keeping,
We'll say, "The feast of Baby's sleeping."

Lullaby, lullaby, slumberland bound,
Please sleep soon and please sleep sound;
And in your dreams you're sure to see
A finer feast than ours will be.

TRADITIONAL JAPANESE NURSERY RHYMES
Adapted by Charlotte B. DeForest

Poems of play and make - believe

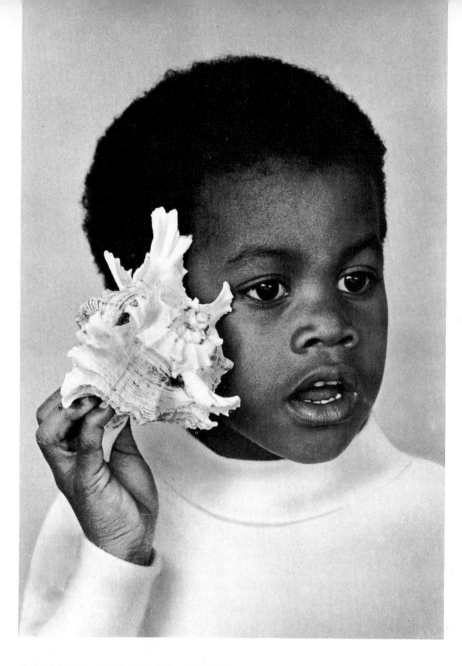

ALONE BY THE SURF

There is no world sound—
Only stillness of stars,
Silence of sand,
A single shell,
By the sliding sea.

LEILA KENDALL BROWN

PALACE

A sea shell is a palace
Where many echoes dwell,
And when I listen to them
I know them all quite well.
They are like the ocean's roar
Where the sea shell buried deep
Learns why the sea is always salt,
And spooky shadows creep.

DOROTHY VENA JOHNSON

sniff

When school is out, we love to follow
our noses over hill and hollow,
smelling jewelweed and vetch,
sniffing fern and milkweed patch.

The airy fifth of our five senses
leads us under, over, fences.
We run like rabbits through bright hours
and poke our noses into flowers!

FRANCES FROST

my nose

It doesn't breathe;
It doesn't smell;
It doesn't feel
So very well.

I am discouraged
With my nose:
The only thing it
Does is blows.

DOROTHY ALDIS

smells

Through all the frozen winter
My nose has grown most lonely
For lovely, lovely, colored smells
That come in springtime only.

The purple smell of lilacs,
The yellow smell that blows
Across the air of meadows
Where bright forsythia grows.

The tall pink smell of peach trees,
The low white smell of clover,
And everywhere the great green smell
Of grass the whole world over.

KATHRYN WORTH

LITTLE

I am the sister of him
And he is my brother.
He is too little for us
To talk to each other.

So every morning I show him
My doll and my book;
But every morning he still is
Too little to look.

DOROTHY ALDIS

THE END

When I was One,
I had just begun.

When I was Two,
I was nearly new.

When I was Three,
I was hardly Me.

When I was Four,
I was not much more.

When I was Five,
I was just alive.

But now I am Six, I'm clever as clever.
So I think I'll be six now for ever and ever.

A. A. MILNE

COUNTING

To count myself
Is quickly done.
There's never more of me
Than one.

KARLA KUSKIN

152

THREE GUESTS

I had a little tea party,
This afternoon at three;
'Twas very small,
Three guests in all,
Just I, myself, and me.

Myself ate up the sandwiches,
While I drank up the tea,
'Twas also I
Who ate the pie
And passed the cake to me.

JESSICA NELSON NORTH

HIDING

I'm hiding, I'm hiding,
And no one knows where;
For all they can see is my
    Toes and my hair.

And I just heard my father
Say to my mother—
"But, darling, he must be
    Somewhere or other.

"Have you looked in the inkwell?"
And Mother said, "Where?"
"In the INKWELL," said Father. But
    I was not there.

Then "Wait!" cried my mother—
"I think that I see
Him under the carpet." But
    It was not me.

"Inside the mirror's
A pretty good place,"
Said Father and looked, but saw
    Only his face.

"We've hunted," sighed Mother,
"As hard as we could
And I AM so afraid that we've
    Lost him for good."

Then I laughed out aloud
And I wiggled my toes
And Father said—"Look, dear,
    I wonder if those

"Toes could be Benny's.
There are ten of them. See?"
And they WERE so surprised to find
    Out it was me!

DOROTHY ALDIS

"SH"

"Sh!" says Mother,
"Sh!" says Father.
"Running in the hall
Is a very great bother."

    "Mrs. Grumpy Grundy,
    Who lives down below,
    Will come right up
    First thing you know."

        "Sh!" says Father,
        "Sh!" says Mother.
        "Can't you play a quiet game
        Of some kind or other?"

JAMES S. TIPPETT   **155**

MERRY-GO-ROUND

I climbed up on the merry-go-round,
And it went round and round.

I climbed up on a big brown horse,
And it went up and down.

    Around and round
    And up and down,
    Around and round
    And up and down.

I sat high up
On a big brown horse
And rode around
On the merry-go-round
    And rode around

On the merry-go-round
I rode around
    On the merry-go-round
    Around and round
    And round.

DOROTHY W. BARUCH

THE ROSE ON MY CAKE

I went to a party,
A party for Pearly,
With presents and ice cream,
With favors and games.
I stayed very late
And I got there quite early.
I met all the guests
And I know all their names.
We sang and we jumped.
We jumped and we jostled.
We jostled and rustled
At musical chairs.
We ate up the cake
And we folded the candy in baskets
In napkins
We folded in squares.
We blew up balloons
And we danced without shoes.
We danced on the floor
And the rug and the bed.
We tripped and we trotted
In trios and twos.
And I neatly balanced myself
On my head.
Pearly just smiled
As she blew out the candles.
I gave the rose from my cake
To a friend,
Millicent Moss,
In her black patent sandals.
The trouble with parties is
All of them end.

KARLA KUSKIN

HAPPY BIRTHDAY

Here's your birthday,
Wrapped with sky
And tied with windy strings.

It's garlanded
With red balloons
And stuck with tiny wings.

It's bigger than
Your arms can hold
But fits you like a glove—

A birthday made
Of woven gold
And buttoned on with love.

BARBARA JUSTER ESBENSEN

A VISIT FROM ST. NICHOLAS

TWAS the night before Christmas, when all through
  the house
Not a creature was stirring, not even a mouse;
The stockings were hung by the chimney with care,
In hopes that St. Nicholas soon would be there;
The children were nestled all snug in their beds,
While visions of sugar-plums danced in their heads;
And mamma in her 'kerchief, and I in my cap,
Had just settled our brains for a long winter's nap,
When out on the lawn there arose such a clatter,
I sprang from the bed to see what was the matter.
Away to the window I flew like a flash,
Tore open the shutters and threw up the sash.
The moon on the breast of the new-fallen snow
Gave the luster of mid-day to objects below,
When, what to my wondering eyes should appear,
But a miniature sleigh, and eight tiny reindeer,
With a little old driver, so lively and quick,
I knew in a moment it must be St. Nick.
More rapid than eagles his coursers they came,
And he whistled, and shouted, and called them by name:
"Now, *Dasher!* now, *Dancer!* now, *Prancer* and *Vixen!*
On, *Comet!* on, *Cupid!* on, *Donder* and *Blitzen!*
To the top of the porch! to the top of the wall!
Now dash away! dash away! dash away all!"
As dry leaves that before the wild hurricane fly,

When they meet with an obstacle, mount to the sky,
So up to the house-top the coursers they flew,
With the sleigh full of toys, and St. Nicholas too.
And then, in a twinkling, I heard on the roof
The prancing and pawing of each little hoof.
As I drew in my head, and was turning around,
Down the chimney St. Nicholas came with a bound.
He was dressed all in fur, from his head to his foot,
And his clothes were all tarnished with ashes and soot;
A bundle of toys he had flung on his back,
And he looked like a peddler just opening his pack.
His eyes—how they twinkled! his dimples how merry!
His cheeks were like roses, his nose like a cherry!
His droll little mouth was drawn up like a bow,
And the beard of his chin was as white as the snow;
The stump of a pipe he held tight in his teeth,
And the smoke it encircled his head like a wreath;
He had a broad face and a little round belly,
That shook, when he laughed, like a bowlful of jelly.
He was chubby and plump, a right jolly old elf,
And I laughed when I saw him, in spite of myself;
A wink of his eye and a twist of his head,
Soon gave me to know I had nothing to dread;
He spoke not a word, but went straight to his work,
And filled all the stockings; then turned with a jerk,
And laying his finger aside of his nose,
And giving a nod, up the chimney he rose;
He sprang to his sleigh, to his team gave a whistle,
And away they all flew like the down of a thistle.
But I heard him exclaim, ere he drove out of sight,
"Happy Christmas to all, and to all a good-night."

CLEMENT CLARKE MOORE

KITE DAYS

A kite, a sky, and a good firm breeze,
And acres of ground away from trees,
And one hundred yards of clean, strong string—
O boy, O boy! I call that Spring!

MARK SAWYER

SLIDING

Down the slide
We ride, we ride.
Round we run, and then
Up we pop
To reach the top,
Down we come again.

MARCHETTE CHUTE

HOPPITY

Christopher Robin goes
Hoppity, hoppity,

Hoppity, hoppity, hop.
Whenever I tell him
Politely to stop it, he
Says he can't possibly stop.

If he stopped hopping, he couldn't go anywhere,
Poor little Christopher
Couldn't go anywhere . . .
That's why he *always* goes
Hoppity, hoppity,
Hoppity,
Hoppity,
Hop.

A. A. MILNE

THE PICNIC

We brought a rug for sitting on,
Our lunch was in a box.
The sand was warm. We didn't wear
Hats or shoes or socks.

Waves came curling up the beach.
We waded. It was fun.
Our sandwiches were different kinds.
I dropped my jelly one.

DOROTHY ALDIS

THE PASTURE

I'm going out to clean the pasture spring;
I'll only stop to rake the leaves away
(And wait to watch the water clear, I may):
I sha'n't be gone long.—You come too.

I'm going out to fetch the little calf
That's standing by the mother. It's so young,
It totters when she licks it with her tongue.
I sha'n't be gone long.—You come too.

ROBERT FROST

SHORE

Play on the seashore
And gather up shells,
Kneel in the damp sands
Digging wells.

Run on the rocks
Where the seaweed slips,
Watch the waves
And the beautiful ships.

MARY BRITTON MILLER

drinking
fountain

When I climb up
To get a drink,
It doesn't work
The way you'd think.

I turn it up.
The water goes
And hits me right
Upon the nose.

I turn it down
To make it small
And don't get any
Drink at all.

MARCHETTE CHUTE

sprinkling

Sometimes in the summer
When the day is hot
Daddy takes the garden hose
And finds a shady spot;
Then he calls me over,
Looks at my bare toes
And says, "Why, you need sprinkling,
You thirsty little rose!"

DOROTHY MASON PIERCE

mud

Mud is very nice to feel
All squishy-squash between the toes!
I'd rather wade in wiggly mud
Than smell a yellow rose.

Nobody else but the rosebush knows
How nice mud feels
Between the toes.

POLLY CHASE BOYDEN

skating

When I try to skate,
My feet are so wary
They grit and they grate:
And then I watch Mary
Easily gliding,
Like an ice fairy;
Skimming and curving,
Out and in,
With a turn of her head,
And a lift of her chin,
And a gleam of her eye,
And a twirl and a spin;
Sailing under
The breathless hush
Of the willows, and back
To the frozen rush;
Out to the island
And round the edge,

Skirting the rim
Of the crackling sedge,
Swerving close
To the poplar root,
And round the lake
On a single foot,
With a three, and an eight,
And a loop and a ring;
Where Mary glides,
The lake will sing!
Out in the mist
I hear her now
Under the frost
Of the willow bough
Easily sailing,
Light and fleet,
With the song of the lake
Beneath her feet.

HERBERT ASQUITH

169

the land of counterpane

When I was sick and lay a-bed,
I had two pillows at my head,
And all my toys beside me lay
To keep me happy all the day.

And sometimes for an hour or so
I watched my leaden soldiers go,
With different uniforms and drills,
Among the bedclothes, through the hills;

And sometimes sent my ships in fleets
All up and down among the sheets;
Or brought my trees and houses out,
And planted cities all about.

I was the giant great and still
That sits upon the pillow-hill,
And sees before him, dale and plain,
The pleasant land of counterpane.

ROBERT LOUIS STEVENSON

wings
and wheels

Ahoy and ahoy, birds!
We cannot have wings
And feathers and things,
But dashing on wheels
With the wind at our heels
Is almost like flying—
Such joy, birds!

Oho and Oho, birds!
Of course we can't rise
Up and up to the skies;
But skimming and sliding
On rollers, and gliding,
Is almost as jolly,
You know, birds!

NANCY BYRD TURNER

leisure

What is this life if, full of care,
We have no time to stand and stare.

No time to stand beneath the boughs
And stare as long as sheep or cows.

No time to see, when woods we pass,
Where squirrels hide their nuts in grass.

No time to see, in broad daylight,
Streams full of stars, like stars at night.

No time to turn at Beauty's glance,
And watch her feet, how they can dance.

No time to wait till her mouth can
Enrich that smile her eyes began.

A poor life this if, full of care,
We have no time to stand and stare.

WILLIAM HENRY DAVIES

HALFWAY DOWN

Halfway down the stairs
Is a stair
Where I sit.
There isn't any
Other stair
Quite like
It.
I'm not at the bottom,
I'm not at the top;
So this is the stair
Where
I always
Stop.

Halfway up the stairs
Isn't up,
And isn't down.
It isn't in the nursery,
It isn't in the town.
And all sorts of funny thoughts
Run round my head:
"It isn't really
Anywhere!
It's somewhere else
Instead!"

A. A. MILNE

poems
about
pets
and

G

rownups

THE ANIMAL STORE

If I had a hundred dollars to spend,
    Or maybe a little more,
I'd hurry as fast as my legs would go
    Straight to the animal store.

I wouldn't say, "How much for this or that?"
    "What kind of dog is he?"
I'd buy as many as rolled an eye,
    Or wagged a tail at me!

I'd take the hound with the drooping ears
    That sits by himself alone;
Cockers and Cairns and wobbly pups
    For to be my very own.

I might buy a parrot all red and green,
    And the monkey I saw before,
If I had a hundred dollars to spend,
    Or maybe a little more.

RACHEL FIELD

175

MY DOG

His nose is short and scrubby;
   His ears hang rather low;
And he always brings the stick back,
   No matter how far you throw.

He gets spanked rather often
   For things he shouldn't do,
Like lying-on-beds, and barking,
   And eating up shoes when they're new.

He always wants to be going
   Where he isn't supposed to go.
He tracks up the house when it's snowing—
   Oh, puppy, I love you so.

MARCHETTE CHUTE

CHUMS

He sits and begs, he gives a paw,
He is, as you can see,
The finest dog you ever saw,
And he belongs to me.

He follows everywhere I go
And even when I swim.
I laugh because he thinks, you know,
That I belong to him.

But still no matter what we do
We never have a fuss;
And so I guess it must be true
That *we* belong to *us*.

ARTHUR GUITERMAN

Puppy And I

I met a Man as I went walking;
We got talking,
Man and I.
"Where are you going to, Man?" I said
   (I said to the Man as he went by).
"Down to the village, to get some bread.
Will you come with me?" "No, not I."

I met a Horse as I went walking;
We got talking,
Horse and I.
"Where are you going to, Horse, today?"
   (I said to the Horse as he went by).
"Down to the village to get some hay.
Will you come with me?" "No, not I."

I met a Woman as I went walking;
We got talking,
Woman and I.
"Where are you going to, Woman, so early?"
   (I said to the Woman as she went by).
"Down to the village to get some barley.
Will you come with me?" "No, not I."

I met some Rabbits as I went walking;
We got talking,
Rabbits and I.
"Where are you going in your brown fur coats?"
   (I said to the Rabbits as they went by).
"Down to the village to get some oats.
Will you come with us?" "No, not I."

I met a Puppy as I went walking;
We got talking,
Puppy and I.
"Where are you going this nice fine day?"
   (I said to the Puppy as he went by).
"Up in the hills to roll and play."
"*I'll* come with you, Puppy," said I.

A. A. MILNE

179

FORGIVEN

I found a little beetle, so that Beetle was his name,
And I called him Alexander and he answered just the same.
I put him in a match-box, and I kept him all the day . . .
And Nanny let my beetle out—
    Yes, Nanny let my beetle out—
    She went and let my beetle out—
    And Beetle ran away.

She said she didn't mean it, and I never said she did,
She said she wanted matches and she just took off the lid,
She said that she was sorry, but it's difficult to catch
An excited sort of beetle you've mistaken for a match.

She said that she was sorry, and I really mustn't mind,
As there's lots and lots of beetles which she's certain we could find,
If we looked about the garden for the holes where beetles hid—
And we'd get another match-box and write BEETLE on the lid.

We went to all the places which a beetle might be near,
And we made the sort of noises which a beetle likes to hear,
And I saw a kind of something, and I gave a sort of shout:
"A beetle-house and Alexander Beetle coming out!"

It was Alexander Beetle I'm as certain as can be
And he had a sort of look as if he thought it must be ME,
And he had a sort of look as if he thought he ought to say:
"I'm very very sorry that I tried to run away."

And Nanny's very sorry too for you-know-what-she-did,
And she's writing ALEXANDER very blackly on the lid.
So Nan and Me are friends, because it's difficult to catch
An excited Alexander you've mistaken for a match.

A. A. MILNE

THE MYSTERIOUS CAT

I saw a proud, mysterious cat,
I saw a proud, mysterious cat,
Too proud to catch a mouse or rat—
Mew, mew, mew.

But catnip she would eat, and purr,
But catnip she would eat, and purr,
And goldfish she did much prefer—
Mew, mew, mew.

I saw a cat—'twas but a dream,
I saw a cat—'twas but a dream,
Who scorned the slave that brought her cream—
Mew, mew, mew.

Unless the slave were dressed in style,
Unless the slave were dressed in style,
And knelt before her all the while—
Mew, mew, mew.

Did you ever hear of a thing like that?
Did you ever hear of a thing like that?
Did you ever hear of a thing like that?
Oh, what a proud, mysterious cat.
Oh, what a proud, mysterious cat.
Oh, what a proud, mysterious cat.
Mew . . . mew . . . mew.

VACHEL LINDSAY

CAT

The black cat yawns,
Opens her jaws,
Stretches her legs,
And shows her claws.

Then she gets up
And stands on four
Long stiff legs
And yawns some more.

She shows her sharp teeth,
She stretches her lip,
Her slice of a tongue
Turns up at the tip.

Lifting herself
On her delicate toes,
She arches her back
As high as it goes.

She lets herself down
With particular care,
And pads away
With her tail in the air.

MARY BRITTON MILLER

183

QUOITS

In wintertime I have such fun
   When I play quoits with father.
I beat him almost every game.
   He never seems to bother.

He looks at mother and just smiles.
   All this seems strange to me,
For when he plays with grown-up folks,
   He beats them easily.

MARY EFFIE LEE NEWSOME

EVERYBODY SAYS

Everybody says
I look just like my mother.
Everybody says
I'm the image of Aunt Bee
Everybody says
My nose is like my father's.
But *I* want to look like ME!

DOROTHY ALDIS

mommies

MOMMIES
   make you brush your teeth
   and put your old clothes on
   and clean the room
   and call you from the playground
   and fuss at daddies and uncles
   and tuck you in at night
   and kiss you

NIKKI GIOVANNI

WALKING

When Daddy
Walks
With Jean and me,
We have a
Lot of fun
'Cause we can't
Walk as fast
As he,
Unless we
Skip and
Run!
I stretch,
And stretch
My legs so far,
I nearly slip
And fall—
But how
Does Daddy
Take such steps?
He doesn't stretch
At all!

GRACE GLAUBITZ

MISS NORMA JEAN PUGH,
FIRST GRADE TEACHER

Who cares if
Two and two
Are four or five
Or red or blue?
Who cares whether
Six or seven
Come before or after
Ten or eleven?
Who cares if
C-A-T
Spells cat or rat
Or tit or tat
Or ball or bat?
Well, I do
But I didn't
Used to—
Until MISS NORMA JEAN PUGH!
She's terribly old
As people go
Twenty-one-or-five-or-six
Or so
But she makes a person want to
KNOW!

MARY O'NEILL

It's a fish

AT MRS. APPLEBY'S

When frost is shining on the trees,
  It's spring at Mrs. Appleby's.
You smell it in the air before
  You step inside the kitchen door.

Rows of scarlet flowers bloom
  From every window in the room.
And funny little speckled fish
  Are swimming in a china dish.

A tiny bird with yellow wings
  Just sits and sings and sings and SINGS.
Outside when frost is on the trees,
  It's spring at Mrs. Appleby's!

ELIZABETH UPHAM MC WEBB

MISS T.

It's a very odd thing—
  As odd as can be—
That whatever Miss T. eats
  Turns into Miss T.;
Porridge and apples,
  Mince, muffins, and mutton,
Jam, junket, jumbles—
  Not a rap, not a button
It matters; the moment
  They're out of her plate,
Though shared by Miss Butcher
  And sour Mr. Bate;
Tiny and cheerful,
  And neat as can be,
Whatever Miss T. eats
  Turns into Miss T.

WALTER DE LA MARE

THE POSTMAN

The whistling postman swings along.
His bag is deep and wide,
And messages from all the world
Are bundled up inside.

The postman's walking up our street.
Soon now he'll ring my bell.
Perhaps there'll be a letter stamped
in Asia. Who can tell?

AUTHOR UNKNOWN

LIKE ME

A garbage man is a garbage man
Who rattles and bangs the garbage can.

Like me.

A policeman carries a club in his hand.

Like me.

The mailman carries a bag. Like mine.
And they all of them always have a good time.

Like me.

DOROTHY ALDIS

P'S THE PROUD POLICEMAN

P's the proud Policeman
With buttons polished neat.
He's pleased to put his hand up
When you want to cross the street.
By daylight he protects you;
He protects you through the dark,
And he points the way politely
To the playground or the park.

PHYLLIS MCGINLEY

MY POLICEMAN

He is always standing there
At the corner of the Square;
He is very big and fine
And his silver buttons shine.

All the carts and taxis do
Everything he tells them to,
And the little errand boys
When they pass him make no noise.

Though I seem so very small
I am not afraid at all;
He and I are friends, you see,
And he always smiles at me.

ROSE FYLEMAN

THE
Ice-Cream
MAN

When summer's in the city,
And brick's a blaze of heat,
The Ice-Cream Man with his little cart
Goes trundling down the street.

Beneath his round umbrella,
Oh, what a joyful sight,
To see him fill the cones with mounds
Of cooling brown or white:

Vanilla, chocolate, strawberry,
Or chilly things to drink
From bottles full of frosty fizz,
Green, orange, white, or pink.

His cart might be a flowerbed
Of roses and sweet peas,
The way the children cluster round
As thick as honeybees.

RACHEL FIELD

THE COBBLER

Crooked heels
    And scuffy toes
Are all the kinds
    Of shoes he knows.

He patches up
    The broken places,
Sews the seams
    And shines their faces.

ELEANOR A. CHAFFEE

THE TOLL TAKER

Roll down your window,
Hand the man a dime,
We're coming to the tollbooth
And we're next in line.
Will the man say "thank you"?
Will the man smile?
Won't he even look at us
Just for a while?
    Child, he's busy counting,
    Child, he's making change.
But can't he even look at us?
Life is very strange.

PATRICIA HUBBELL

THE DENTIST

I'd like to be a dentist with a plate upon the door
And a little bubbling fountain in the middle of the floor;
With lots of tiny bottles all arranged in colored rows
And a page boy with a line of silver buttons down his clothes.

I'd love to polish up the things and put them every day
Inside the darling chests of drawers all tidily away;
And every Sunday afternoon when nobody was there
I should go riding up and down upon the velvet chair.

ROSE FYLEMAN

ONLY ONE MOTHER

Hundreds of stars in the pretty sky,
Hundreds of shells on the shore together,
Hundreds of birds that go singing by,
Hundreds of lambs in the sunny weather.

Hundreds of dewdrops to greet the dawn,
Hundreds of bees in the purple clover,
Hundreds of butterflies on the lawn,
But only one mother the wide world over.

GEORGE COOPER

City poems

highway,
byway,
and

MAPS

High adventure
   And bright dream—
Maps are mightier
   Than they seem:

Ships that follow
   Leaning stars—
Red and gold of
   Strange bazaars—

Ice floes hid
   Beyond all knowing—
Planes that ride where
   Winds are blowing!

Train maps, maps of
   Wind and weather,
Road maps—taken
   Altogether

Maps are really
   Magic wands
For home-staying
   Vagabonds!

DOROTHY BROWN THOMPSON

UP IN THE AIR

Zooming across the sky
Like a great bird you fly,
   Airplane,
   Silvery white
   In the light.

Turning and twisting in air,
When shall I ever be there,
   Airplane,
   Piloting you
   Far in the blue?

JAMES S. TIPPETT

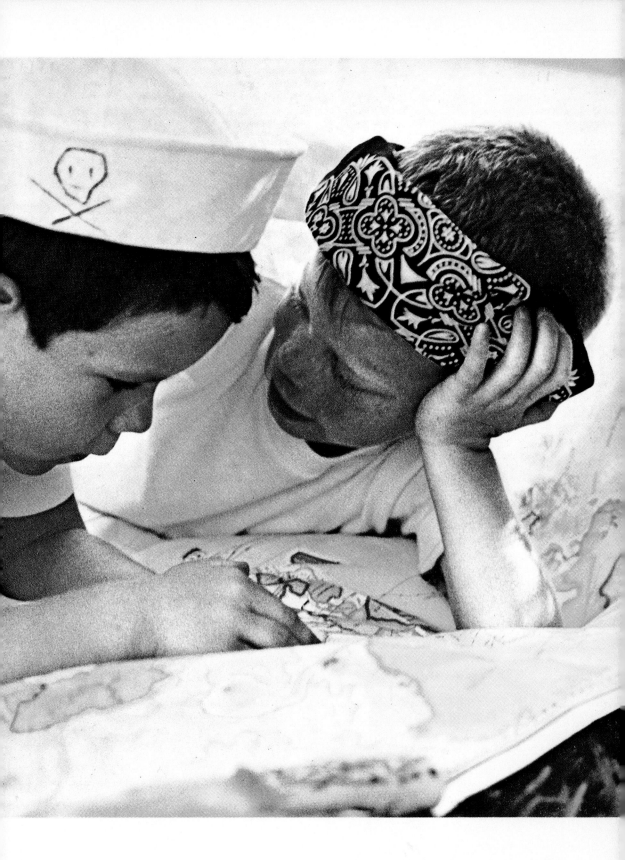

WESTERN WAGONS

They went with axe and rifle,
 when the trail was still to blaze,
They went with wife and children,
 in the prairie-schooner days,
With banjo and with frying pan—
 Susanna, don't you cry!
For I'm off to California
 to get rich out there or die!

We've broken land and cleared it,
 but we're tired of where we are.
They say that wild Nebraska
 is a better place by far.
There's gold in far Wyoming,
 There's black earth in Ioway,
So pack up the kids and blankets,
 for we're moving out today!

The cowards never started
 and the weak died on the road,
And all across the continent
 the endless campfires glowed.
We'd taken land and settled—
 but a traveler passed by—
And we're going West tomorrow—
 Lordy, never ask us why!

We're going West tomorrow,
 where the promises can't fail.
O'er the hills in legions, boys,
 and crowd the dusty trail!
We shall starve and freeze and suffer.
 We shall die, and tame the lands.
But we're going West tomorrow,
 with our fortune in our hands.

STEPHEN VINCENT BENÉT

INDIAN CHILDREN

Where we walk to school each day
Indian children used to play—
All about our native land,
Where the shops and houses stand.

And the trees were very tall,
And there were no streets at all,
Not a church and not a steeple—
Only woods and Indian people.

Only wigwams on the ground,
And at night bears prowling round—
What a different place today
Where we live and work and play!

—ANNETTE WYNNE

STOP - GO

Automobiles
          In
          a
          row
Wait to go
While the signal says:
                    STOP

Bells ring
Ting-a-ling
Red light's gone!
Green light's on!
Horns blow!
And the row
          Starts
                to
                    GO

DOROTHY W. BARUCH

TAXIS

Ho, for taxis green or blue,
   Hi, for taxis red,
They roll along the Avenue
   Like spools of colored thread!

Jack-o'-Lantern yellow,
Orange as the moon,
Greener than the greenest grass
Ever grew in June.
Gaily striped or checked in squares,
Wheels that twinkle bright,
Don't you think that taxis make
A very pleasant sight?
Taxis shiny in the rain,
Scudding through the snow,
Taxis flashing back the sun
Waiting in a row.

Ho, for taxis red and green,
   Hi, for taxis blue,
I wouldn't be a private car
   In sober black, would you?

RACHEL FIELD

GOOD GREEN BUS

Rumbling and rattly good green Bus
Where are you going to carry us?
Up the shiny lengths of Avenue
Where lights keep company two by two;
Where windows glitter with things to buy,
And churches hold their steeples high.
Round the Circle and past the Park,
Still and shadowy, dim and dark,
Over the asphalt and into the Drive—
Isn't it fun to be alive?
Look to the left and the River's there
With ships and whistles and freshened air;
To the right—more windows, row on row,
And everyone like a picture show,
Or little stages where people play
At being themselves by night and day,
And never guess that they have us
For audience in the good green Bus!

RACHEL FIELD

MOTOR CARS

From a city window, 'way up high,
I like to watch the cars go by.
They look like burnished beetles, black,
That leave a little muddy track
Behind them as they slowly crawl.
Sometimes they do not move at all
But huddle close with hum and drone
As though they feared to be alone.
They grope their way through fog and night
With the golden feelers of their light.

ROWENA BASTIN BENNETT

203

CITY STREETS
AND
COUNTRY ROADS

The city has streets—
    But the country has roads.
In the country one meets
    Blue carts with their loads
Of sweet-smelling hay,
    And mangolds, and grain:
Oh, take me away
    To the country again!

In the city one sees
    Big trams rattle by,
And the breath of the chimneys
    That blot out the sky,
And all down the pavements
    Stiff lamp-posts one sees—
But the country has hedgerows,
    The country has trees.

As sweet as the sun
    In the country is rain:
Oh, take me away
    To the country again!

ELEANOR FARJEON

COUNTRY TRUCKS

Big trucks with apples
And big trucks with grapes
Thundering through the mountains
While every wild thing gapes.

Thundering through the valley,
Like something just let loose,
Big trucks with oranges
For city children's juice.

Big trucks with peaches,
And big trucks with pears,
Frightening all the rabbits
And giving squirrels gray hairs.

Yet, when city children
Sit down to plum or prune,
They know more trucks are coming
As surely as the moon.

MONICA SHANNON

THE WAYS OF TRAINS

I hear the engine pounding
in triumph down the track—
trains take away the ones you love
and then they bring them back!

trains take away the ones you love
to worlds both strange and new
and then, with care and courtesy,
they bring them back to you.

The engine halts and snuffs and snorts,
it breathes forth smoke and fire,
then snatches crowded strangers on—
but leaves what you desire!

ELIZABETH COATSWORTH

A MODERN DRAGON

A train is a dragon that roars through the dark,
He wriggles his tail as he sends up a spark.
He pierces the night with his one yellow eye,
And all the earth trembles when he rushes by.

ROWENA BASTIN BENNETT

TRAINS AT NIGHT

I like the whistle of trains at night,
The fast trains thundering by so proud!
They rush and rumble across the world,
They ring wild bells and they toot so loud!

But I love better the slow trains.
They take their time through the world instead,
And whistle softly and stop to tuck
Each sleepy blinking town in bed!

FRANCES FROST

THE RIVER IS A
PIECE OF SKY

From the top of a bridge
The river below
Is a piece of sky—
    Until you throw
    A penny in
    Or a cockleshell
    Or a pebble or two
    Or a bicycle bell
    Or a cobblestone
    Or a fat man's cane—
And then you can see
It's a river again.

The difference you'll see
When you drop your penny:
The river has splashes,
The sky hasn't any.

JOHN CIARDI

HOW TO TELL
THE TOP OF A HILL

The top of a hill
Is not until
The bottom is below.
And you have to stop
When you reach the top
For there's no more UP to go.

To make it plain
Let me explain:
The one *most* reason why
You have to stop
When you reach the top—is:
The next step up is sky.

JOHN CIARDI

I'D LIKE TO BE A LIGHTHOUSE

I'd like to be a lighthouse
All scrubbed and painted white.
I'd like to be a lighthouse
And stay awake all night
To keep my eye on everything
That sails my patch of sea;
I'd like to be a lighthouse
With the ships all watching me.

RACHEL FIELD

WHERE GO THE BOATS?

Dark brown is the river
 Golden is the sand.
It flows along forever,
 With trees on either hand.

Green leaves a-floating,
 Castles of the foam,
Boats of mine a-boating—
 Where will all come home?

On goes the river
 And out past the mill,
Away down the valley,
 Away down the hill.

Away down the river,
 A hundred miles or more.
Other little children
 Shall bring my boats ashore.

ROBERT LOUIS STEVENSON

JAPANESE HAIKU

I must go begging
for water . . . morning glories
have captured my well.

CHIYO

How cool cut hay smells
when carried through the farm gate
as the sun comes up!

BONCHO

What a wonderful
day! No one in the village
doing anything.

SHIKI

Under the willow
With a leaf stuck in his mouth
The puppy sleeps.

ISSA

211

BUILDING A SKYSCRAPER

They're building a skyscraper
Near our street.
Its height will be nearly
One thousand feet.

It covers completely
A city block.
They drilled its foundation
Through solid rock.

They made its framework
Of great steel beams
With riveted joints
And welded seams.

A swarm of workmen
Strain and strive
Like busy bees
In a honeyed hive

Building the skyscraper
Into the air
While crowds of people
Stand and stare.

Higher and higher
The tall towers rise
Like Jacob's ladder
Into the skies.

JAMES S. TIPPETT

CITY

In the morning the city
Spreads its wings
Making a song
In stone that sings.

In the evening the city
Goes to bed
Hanging lights
About its head.

LANGSTON HUGHES

SNOWY MORNING

Wake
gently this morning
to a different day.
Listen.

There is no bray
of buses,
no brake growls,
no siren howls and
no horns
blow.
There is only
the silence
of a city
hushed
by snow.

LILIAN MOORE

SKYSCRAPER IS A CITY'S HOUSE

Skyscraper is a City's house
Only a city would need to build a house to reach the clouds
Only a city would dare to raise a building twelve hundred
feet into the air
Only a city of many roads could summon stone and cement,
chromium and steel
Only a city of myriad workers could fashion the complex giant,
could rear a house of a hundred stories in twenty months,
a house strong to shelter eighty thousand people.
SKYSCRAPER is a city's house!

ELSA NAUMBURG, CLARA LAMBERT, AND LUCY SPRAGUE MITCHELL

ELEVATOR →

the ELEVATOR

The elevator
In the store
Has a door
That slides
Open—closed.

Then the driver moves a handle,
And up and up
The elevator slips
And *stops*
And *out* go some people
And *in* come some people.

And up and up the elevator slips
And stops
And out go some people
And in come some people.
And down and *down*
The elevator drops
To the floor
Where I
Get out.

DOROTHY W. BARUCH

EXIT →

214

E is the ESCALATOR

E is the Escalator
   That gives an elegant ride.
You step on the stair
With an easy air
   And up and up you glide.
It's nicer than scaling ladders
   Or scrambling 'round a hill,
For you climb and climb
But all the time
You're really standing still.

PHYLLIS McGINLEY

215

THE TELEGRAPH

The wires spread out far and wide,
And cross the town and countryside,
They cross through deserts and through snows,
And pass the spots where no one goes.

But though no feet go out that way
A million words go every day;
Along the wires everywhere
A million words flash through the air.

And if we're happy, if we're well,
The wires far away can tell,
The little words can cross all space
And talk to friends in any place.

ANNETTE WYNNE

A LETTER
IS A GYPSY ELF

A letter is a gypsy elf
It goes where I would go myself;
East or West or North, it goes,
Or South past pretty bungalows,
Over mountain, over hill,
Any place it must and will,
It finds good friends that live so far
You cannot travel where they are.

ANNETTE WYNNE

MAIL

Writing a letter
    Is really quite fun
Because I can mail it
    As soon as it's done.

MARCHETTE CHUTE

THE WORLD

Great, wide, beautiful,
  wonderful World,
With the wonderful water
  round you curled,
And the wonderful grass
  upon your breast,
World, you are beautifully drest.

WILLIAM BRIGHTY RANDS

OTHERWISE

There must be magic,
Otherwise,
How could day turn to night,

And how could sailboats,
Otherwise,
Go sailing out of sight,

And how could peanuts,
Otherwise,
Be covered up so tight?

AILEEN FISHER

Verses just for fun

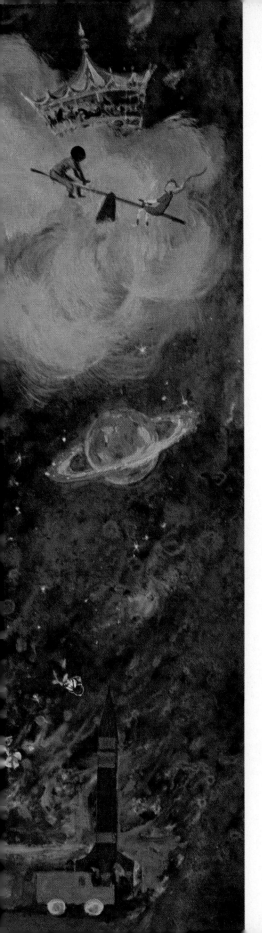

THE LITTLE LAND

When at home alone I sit,
And am very tired of it,
I have just to shut my eyes
To go sailing through the skies—
To go sailing far away
To the pleasant Land of Play.

ROBERT LOUIS STEVENSON

LAUGHING SONG

Come live and be merry,
            and join with me,
To sing the sweet chorus
            of "Ha, ha, he!"

WILLIAM BLAKE

221

CIRCLES

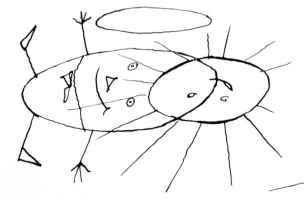

The things to draw with compasses
Are suns and moons and circleses
And rows of humptydumpasses
Or anything in circuses
Like hippopotamusseses
And hoops and camels' humpasses
And wheels on clownses busseses
And fat old elephumpasses.

HARRY BEHN

THE VULTURE

The Vulture eats between his meals,
  And that's the reason why
He very, very rarely feels
  As well as you and I.
His eye is dull, his head is bald,
  His neck is growing thinner.
Oh! what a lesson for us all
  To only eat at dinner!

HILAIRE BELLOC

THE PURPLE COW

I never Saw a Purple Cow,
I never Hope to See One;
But I can Tell you, Anyhow,
I'd rather See than Be One.

GELETT BURGESS

HORSIES MAKE HORSIES

Horsies make horsies
And ants make ants.
And elephants
Make elephants.
But bees make honey,
Isn't it funny?

JOHN LEONARD BECKER

223

LIMERICKS

There Was an Old Person of Ware

There was an old person of Ware,
Who rode on the back of a bear;
When they said, "Does it trot?"
He said: "Certainly not,
It's a Moppsikon Floppsikon bear."

EDWARD LEAR

There Was an Old Man with a Beard

There was an old man with a beard,
Who said, "It is just as I feared!
Two Owls and a Hen
Four Larks and a Wren
Have all built their nests in my beard."

EDWARD LEAR

There Was a Young Maid Who Said, "Why"

There was a young maid who said, "Why
Can't I look in my ear with my eye?
If I give my mind to it,
I'm sure I can do it,
You never can tell till you try."

EDWARD LEAR

ELETELEPHONY

Once there was an elephant,
Who tried to use the telephant—
No! no! I mean an elephone
Who tried to use the telephone—
(Dear me! I am not certain quite
That even now I've got it right.)

Howe'er it was, he got his trunk
Entangled in the telephunk;
The more he tried to get it free,
The louder buzzed the telephee—
(I fear I'd better drop the song
Of elephop and telephong!)

LAURA E. RICHARDS

THE OWL AND THE PUSSYCAT

The Owl and the Pussycat went to sea
In a beautiful pea-green boat,
They took some honey, and plenty of money,
Wrapped up in a five-pound note.
The Owl looked up to the stars above,
And sang to a small guitar,
"O lovely Pussy! O Pussy, my love,
What a beautiful Pussy you are,
You are,
You are!
What a beautiful Pussy you are!"

Pussy said to the Owl, "You elegant fowl!
How charmingly sweet you sing!
O let us be married! too long we have tarried:
But what shall we do for a ring?"
They sailed away for a year and a day,
To the land where the Bong-tree grows;
And there in a wood a Piggy-wig stood,
With a ring at the end of his nose,
His nose,
His nose,
With a ring at the end of his nose.

"Dear Pig, are you willing to sell for one shilling
Your ring?" Said the Piggy, "I will."
So they took it away, and were married next day
By the Turkey who lives on the hill.
They dined on mince, and slices of quince,
Which they ate with a runcible spoon;
And hand in hand, on the edge of the sand,
They danced by the light of the moon,
The moon,
The moon,
They danced by the light of the moon.

EDWARD LEAR

I Speak,
I Say,
I Talk

Cats purr.
Lions roar.
Owls hoot.
Bears snore.
Crickets creak.
Mice squeak.
Sheep baa.
But I SPEAK!

Monkeys chatter.
Cows moo.
Ducks quack.
Doves coo.
Pigs squeal.
Horses neigh.
Chickens cluck.
But I SAY!

Flies hum.
Dogs growl.
Bats screech.
Coyotes howl.
Frogs croak.
Parrots squawk.
Bees buzz.
But I TALK!

ARNOLD L. SHAPIRO

TWENTY FROGGIES

Twenty froggies went to school
Down beside a rushy pool.
Twenty little coats of green,
Twenty vests all white and clean.

"We must be in time," said they,
"First we study, then we play.
That is how we keep the rule,
When we froggies go to school."

Master Bullfrog, brave and stern,
Called his classes in their turn,
Taught them how to nobly strive,
Also how to leap and dive;

Taught them how to dodge a blow
From the sticks that bad boys throw.
Twenty froggies grew up fast,
Bullfrogs they became at last;

Polished in a high degree,
As each froggie ought to be,
Now they sit on other logs,
Teaching other little frogs.

GEORGE COOPER

ROAD FELLOWS

Little Tillie Turtle
Went a-walking down the road
And happened at the corner
On little Tommy Toad.
"Good-morning, Sir," said Tillie.
"Good-morning, Ma'am," said he,
And they strolled along together
As cosy as could be.

And when they reached the orchard,
As sure as you're alive,
They saw big Billy Bumble-bee
Emerging from his hive.
"Good-morning, friends," said Billy.
"Good-morning, Sir," said they.
"We're very glad to notice
That you're going down our way."

Along they sauntered gaily,
Till on a wayside stone
They saw young Benny Beetle Bug
A-sitting there alone.
"Good-morning, Sir," they caroled.
"Good-morning all, to you,"
Said Benny, "are you traveling?
I'd like to travel, too."
They beckoned him politely;
He followed with a will.
And if they haven't stopped for tea
I think they're strolling still.

BARBARA YOUNG

THERE ONCE WAS A PUFFIN

Oh, there once was a Puffin
Just the shape of a muffin,
And he lived on an island
   In the
      bright
        blue
          sea!

He ate little fishes,
That were most delicious,
And he had them for supper
   And he
      had them
        for tea.

But this poor little Puffin,
He couldn't play nothin',
For he hadn't anybody
   To
      play
        with
          at all.

So he sat on his island,
And he cried for awhile, and
He felt very lonely,
   And he
      felt
        very
          small.

Then along came the fishes,
And they said, "If you wishes,
You can have us for playmates,
   Instead
      of
        for
          tea!"

So they now play together,
In all sorts of weather,
And the Puffin eats pancakes,
   Like you
      and
        like
          me.

FLORENCE PAGE JAQUES

THE DUEL

The gingham dog and the calico cat
Side by side on the table sat;
'Twas half-past twelve, and (what do you think!)
Nor one nor t'other had slept a wink!
The old Dutch clock and the Chinese plate
Appeared to know as sure as fate
There was going to be a terrible spat.
(*I wasn't there; I simply state*
What was told to me by the Chinese plate!)

The gingham dog went, "Bow-wow-wow!"
And the calico cat replied, "Mee-ow!"
The air was littered, an hour or so,
With bits of gingham and calico,
While the old Dutch clock in the chimney place
Up with its hands before its face,
For it always dreaded a family row!
(*Now mind: I'm only telling you*
What the old Dutch clock declares is true!)

The Chinese plate looked very blue,
And wailed, "Oh, dear! what shall we do!"
But the gingham dog and the calico cat
Wallowed this way and tumbled that,
Employing every tooth and claw
In the awfullest way you ever saw—
And, oh! how the gingham and calico flew!
(*Don't fancy I exaggerate—*
I got my news from the Chinese plate!)

Next morning, where the two had sat,
They found no trace of dog or cat;
And some folks think unto this day
That burglars stole that pair away!
But the truth about the cat and pup
Is this: they ate each other up!
Now what do you really think of that!
(*The old Dutch clock it told me so,*
And that is how I came to know.)

EUGENE FIELD

I SAW A SHIP A-SAILING

I saw a ship a-sailing,
A-sailing on the sea;
And, oh! it was all laden
With pretty things for thee!

There were comfits in the cabin,
And apples in the hold.
The sails were all of silk,
And the masts were made of gold.

The four-and-twenty sailors
That stood between the decks,
Were four-and-twenty white mice,
With chains about their necks.

The captain was a duck,
With a packet on his back;
And when the ship began to move,
The captain said, "Quack! Quack!"

OLD RHYME

TOUCANS TWO

Whatever one toucan can do
is sooner done by toucans two,
and three toucans (it's very true)
can do much more than two can do.

And toucans numbering two plus two can
manage more than all the zoo can.
In short, there is no toucan who can
do what four or three or two can.

JACK PRELUTSKY

THE HUMMINGBIRD

The ruby-throated hummingbird
is hardly bigger than this WORD.

JACK PRELUTSKY

BEES

Every bee
that
ever was
was
partly
sting
and partly
. . . buzz.

JACK PRELUTSKY

HE THOUGHT HE SAW

He thought he saw a Buffalo
Upon the chimney piece:
He looked again, and found it was
His Sister's Husband's Niece.
"Unless you leave this house!"
  he said,
"I'll send for the Police!"

He thought he saw a Banker's Clerk
Descending from the bus:
He looked again, and found it was
A Hippopotamus.
"If this should stay to dine," he said,
"There won't be much for us!"

He thought he saw an Albatross
That fluttered round the lamp:
He looked again, and found it was
A Penny-Postage-Stamp.
"You'd best be getting home," he said:
"The nights are very damp!"

LEWIS CARROLL

MR. NOBODY

I know a funny little man,
   As quiet as a mouse,
Who does the mischief that is done
   In everybody's house!
There's no one ever sees his face,
   And yet we all agree
That every plate we break was cracked
   By Mr. Nobody.

'Tis he who always tears our books,
   Who leaves the door ajar,
He pulls the buttons from our shirts,
   And scatters pins afar;
That squeaking door will always squeak,
   For, prithee, don't you see,
We leave the oiling to be done
   By Mr. Nobody.

He puts damp wood upon the fire,
   That kettles cannot boil;
His are the feet that bring in mud,
   And all the carpets soil.
The papers always are mislaid,
   Who had them last but he?
There's no one tosses them about
   But Mr. Nobody.

The finger marks upon the door
   By none of us are made;
We never leave the blinds unclosed,
   To let the curtains fade.
The ink we never spill; the boots
   That lying round you see
Are not our boots—they all belong
   To Mr. Nobody.

AUTHOR UNKNOWN

MRS. SNIPKIN AND MRS. WOBBLECHIN

Skinny Mrs. Snipkin,
    With her little pipkin,
Sat by the fireside a-warming of her toes.
    Fat Mrs. Wobblechin,
    With her little doublechin,
Sat by the window a-cooling of her nose.

Says this one to that one,
    "Oh! you silly fat one,
Will you shut the window down?
You're freezing me to death!"
Says that one to t'other one,
    "Good gracious,
    how you bother one!
There isn't air enough for me
to draw my precious breath!"

Skinny Mrs. Snipkin,
Took her little pipkin,
Threw it straight across the room
    as hard as she could throw;
Hit Mrs. Wobblechin
On her little doublechin
    And out of the window
    a-tumble she did go.

LAURA E. RICHARDS

JONATHAN BING

Poor old Jonathan Bing
Went out in his carriage to visit the King,
But everyone pointed and said, "Look at that!
Jonathan Bing has forgotten his hat!"
    (He'd forgotten his hat!)

Poor old Jonathan Bing
Went home and put on a new hat for the King,
But by the palace a soldier said, "Hi!
You can't see the King; you've forgotten your tie!"
    (He'd forgotten his tie!)

Poor old Jonathan Bing,
He put on a beautiful tie for the King,
But when he arrived, an Archbishop said, "Ho!
You can't come to court in pajamas, you know!"

Poor old Jonathan Bing
Went home and addressed a short note to the King:
"If you please will excuse me, I won't come to tea;
For home's the best place for all people like me!"

BEATRICE CURTIS BROWN

THE RAGGEDY MAN

O the Raggedy Man! He works fer Pa;
An' he's the goodest man ever you saw!
He comes to our house every day,
An' waters the horses, an' feeds 'em hay;
An' he opens the shed—an' we all ist laugh
When he drives out our little old wobble-ly calf;
An' nen—ef our hired girl says he can—
He milks the cow fer 'Lizabuth Ann—
Ain't he a' awful good Raggedy Man?
　　Raggedy! Raggedy! Raggedy Man!

Why, the Raggedy Man—he's ist so good
He splits the kindlin' an' chops the wood;
An' nen he spades in our garden, too,
An' does most things 'at *boys* can't do!—
He clumbed clean up in our big tree
An' shooked a' apple down fer me—
An' nother'n', too, fer 'Lizabuth Ann—
An' nother'n', too, fer the Raggedy Man—
Ain't he a' awful kind Raggedy Man?
　　Raggedy! Raggedy! Raggedy Man!

An' the Raggedy Man, he knows most rhymes
An' tells 'em, ef I be good, sometimes;
Knows 'bout Giunts, an' Griffuns, an' Elves,
An' the Squidgicum-Squees 'at swallers therselves!
An' wite by the pump in our pasture-lot,
He showed me the hole 'at the Wunks is got,
'At lives 'way deep in the ground, an' can
Turn into me, er 'Lizabuth Ann!
Er Ma, er Pa, er the Raggedy Man!
Ain't he a funny old Raggedy Man?
　　Raggedy! Raggedy! Raggedy Man!

The Raggedy Man—one time when he
Was makin' a little bow-'n'-arry fer me,
Says, "When *you're* big like your Pa is,
Air you go' to keep a fine store like his—
An' be a rich merchunt—an' wear fine clothes?—
Er what *air* you go' to be, goodness knows!"
An' nen he laughed at 'Lizabuth Ann,
An' I says, "'M go' to be a Raggedy Man!—
I'm ist go' to be a nice Raggedy Man!"
　　Raggedy! Raggedy! Raggedy Man!

JAMES WHITCOMB RILEY

247

Pirate Don Durk of Dowdee

Ho, for the Pirate Don Durk of Dowdee!
He was as wicked as wicked could be,
But, oh, he was perfectly gorgeous to see!
The Pirate Don Durk of Dowdee.

His conscience, of course, was as black as a bat,
But he had a floppety plume on his hat
And when he went walking it jiggled—like that!
The plume of the Pirate Dowdee.

His coat it was handsome and cut with a slash,
And often as ever he twirled his mustache
Deep down in the ocean the mermaids went splash,
  Because of Don Durk of Dowdee.

Moreover, Dowdee had a purple tattoo,
And stuck in his belt where he buckled it through
Were a dagger, a dirk, and a squizzamaroo,
  For fierce was the Pirate Dowdee.

So fearful he was he would shoot at a puff,
And always at sea when the weather grew rough
He drank from a bottle and wrote on his cuff,
  Did Pirate Don Durk of Dowdee.

Oh, he had a cutlass that swung at his thigh
And he had a parrot called Pepperkin Pye,
And a zigzaggy scar at the end of his eye
  Had Pirate Don Durk of Dowdee.

He kept in a cavern, this buccaneer bold,
A curious chest that was covered with mould,
And all of his pockets were jingly with gold!
  Oh, jing! went the gold of Dowdee.

His conscience, of course, it was crook'd like a squash,
But both of his boots made a slickery slosh,
And he went through the world with a wonderful swash,
  Did Pirate Don Durk of Dowdee.

It's true he was wicked as wicked could be,
His sins they outnumbered a hundred and three,
But, oh, he was perfectly gorgeous to see,
  The Pirate Don Durk of Dowdee.

MILDRED PLEW MEIGS

LITTLE JOE TUNNEY

There was a little boy
And his name was Joe Tunney.
He had but one failing:
He tried to be funny.

He made himself noticed
In all public places
By making loud noises
And terrible faces.

One day at the circus
He wouldn't sit down.
He stood up and tried
To perform like a clown.

The clown said, "All right,
If you must jump and sing,
Come out with the show
And perform in the ring."

So out ran young Joe,
Acting foolish and wild,
And everyone watched him
But nobody smiled.

The actors all watched him,
The band loudly blared.
In dignified silence
The animals stared.

Thought poor little Joe,
Standing lonely and small,
"Oh, what shall I do?
I'm not funny at all!"

Then the elephant spoke
In the elephant tongue,
"I'll help that boy out—
After all, he's so young."

And he lifted Joe up
With his trunk in the air
And with one mighty sweep
Put him back in his chair.

The people all clapped
And the clowns cheered for Joe,
And he kept very still
For the rest of the show.

REBECCA MC CANN

THE CAVE BOY

I dreamed I was a cave boy
    And lived in a cave,
A mammoth for my saddle horse,
    A monkey for my slave.
And through the tree-fern forests
    A-riding I would go,
When I was once a cave boy,
    A million years ago.

I dreamed I was a cave boy;
    I hunted with a spear
The saber-toothèd tiger,
    The prehistoric deer.
A wolfskin for my dress suit,
    I thought me quite a beau,
When I was once a cave boy,
    A million years ago.

I dreamed I was a cave boy;
    My dinner was a bone,
And how I had to fight for it,
    To get it for my own!
We banged each other o'er the head,
    And oft our blood did flow,
When I was once a cave boy,
    A million years ago.

I dreamed I was a cave boy.
    The torches' smoky light
Shone on the dinner table,
    A pile of bones so white.
I lapped some water from the spring,
    The easiest way, you know,
When I was once a cave boy,
    A million years ago.

I dreamed—but now I am awake;
    A voice is in my ear.
"Come out and have a game of ball!
    The sun is shining clear.
We'll have some doughnuts afterwards,
    And then a-swimming go!"
I'm glad I'm *not* a cave boy,
    A million years ago!

LAURA E. RICHARDS

253

THE SUGAR-PLUM TREE

Have you ever heard of the Sugar-Plum Tree?
    'Tis a marvel of great renown!
It blooms on the shore of the Lollipop Sea
    In the garden of Shut-Eye Town;
The fruit that it bears is so wondrously sweet
    (As those who have tasted it say)
That good little children have only to eat
    Of that fruit to be happy next day.

When you've got to the tree, you would have a hard time
    To capture the fruit which I sing;
The tree is so tall that no person could climb
    To the boughs where the sugar-plums swing!
But up in that tree sits a chocolate cat,
    And a gingerbread dog prowls below—
And this is the way you contrive to get at
    Those sugar-plums tempting you so:

You say but the word to that gingerbread dog
    And he barks with such terrible zest
That the chocolate cat is at once all agog,
    As her swelling proportions attest.
And the chocolate cat goes cavorting around
    From this leafy limb unto that,
And the sugar-plums tumble, of course, to the ground—
    Hurrah for that chocolate cat!

There are marshmallows, gumdrops, and peppermint canes,
    With stripings of scarlet and gold,
And you carry away of the treasure that rains
    As much as your apron can hold!
So come, little child, cuddle closer to me
    In your dainty white nightcap and gown,
And I'll rock you away to that Sugar-Plum Tree
    In the garden of Shut-Eye Town.

EUGENE FIELD

WYNKEN, BLYNKEN, AND NOD

Wynken, Blynken, and Nod one night
Sailed off in a wooden shoe—
Sailed on a river of crystal light
    Into a sea of dew.
"Where are you going, and what do you wish?"
The old moon asked the three.
"We have come to fish for the herring fish
    That live in this beautiful sea;
    Nets of silver and gold have we!"
        Said Wynken,
        Blynken,
        And Nod.

The old moon laughed and sang a song,
As they rocked in the wooden shoe,
And the wind that sped them all night long
    Ruffled the waves of dew.
The little stars were the herring fish
That lived in that beautiful sea—
"Now cast your nets wherever you wish—
    Never afeard are we!"
So cried the stars to the fishermen three:
        Wynken,
        Blynken,
        And Nod.

All night long their nets they threw
To the stars in the twinkling foam—
Then down from the skies came the wooden shoe,
        Bringing the fishermen home;
'Twas all so pretty a sail it seemed
As if it could not be,
And some folks thought 'twas a dream they'd dreamed
        Of sailing that beautiful sea—
        But I shall name you the fishermen three:
                Wynken,
                Blynken,
                And Nod.

Wynken and Blynken are two little eyes,
And Nod is a little head,
And the wooden shoe that sailed the skies
        Is a wee one's trundle-bed.
So shut your eyes while mother sings
Of wonderful sights that be,
And you shall see the beautiful things
        As you rock in the misty sea
Where the old shoe rocked the fishermen three:
                Wynken,
                Blynken,
                And Nod.

EUGENE FIELD

THE LITTLE HOUSE

In a great big wood in a great big tree
There's the nicest little house that could possibly be.

There's a tiny little knocker on the tiny little door,
And a tiny little carpet on the tiny little floor;

There's a tiny little table, and a tiny little bed,
And a tiny little pillow for a tiny *weeny* head;

A tiny little blanket, and a tiny little sheet,
And a tiny water bottle (hot) for tiny little feet.

A tiny little eiderdown; a tiny little chair;
And a tiny little kettle for the owner
(when he's there).

In a tiny little larder there's a tiny thermos bottle
For a tiny little greedy man who knows the
Woods of Pottle.

There's a tiny little peg for a tiny little hat,
And a tiny little dog and a tiny *tiny* cat.

If you've got a little house
And you keep it spick and span,
Perhaps there'll come to live in it
A tiny little man.
You may not ever see him
(He is extremely shy):
But if you find a crumpled sheet,
Or pins upon the window seat,
Or see the marks of tiny feet
You'll know the reason why.

ELIZABETH GODLEY

THE FAIRIES

Up the airy mountain,
 Down the rushy glen,
We daren't go a-hunting
 For fear of little men;
Wee folk, good folk,
 Trooping all together;
Green jacket, red cap,
 And white owl's feather!

Down along the rocky shore
 Some make their home,
They live on crispy pancakes
 Of yellow tide-foam;
Some in the reeds
 Of the black mountain-lake,
With frogs for their watchdogs,
 All night awake.

By the craggy hillside,
 Through the mosses bare,
They have planted thorn trees
 For pleasure, here and there.
Is any man so daring
 As dig them up in spite,
He shall find their sharpest thorns
 In his bed at night.

Up the airy mountain,
 Down the rushy glen,
We daren't go a-hunting
 For fear of little men;
Wee folk, good folk,
 Trooping all together;
Green jacket, red cap,
 And white owl's feather!

WILLIAM ALLINGHAM

Oh, who is so merry, so merry, heigh ho!
As the light-hearted fairy? heigh ho,
      Heigh ho!
  He dances and sings
  To the sound of his wings,
With a hey and a heigh and a ho!

Oh, who is so merry, so airy, heigh ho!
As the light-hearted fairy? heigh ho,
      Heigh ho!
  His nectar he sips
  From the primroses' lips,
With a hey and a heigh and a ho!

Oh, who is so merry, so merry, heigh ho!
As the light-hearted fairy? heigh ho!
      Heigh ho!
  The night is his noon
  And his sun is the moon,
With a hey and a heigh and a ho!

THE LIGHT-HEARTED FAIRY

AUTHOR UNKNOWN

THE BEST GAME THE FAIRIES PLAY

The best game the fairies play,
  The best game of all,
Is sliding down steeples—
  (You know they're very tall).
You fly to the weathercock,
  And when you hear it crow
You fold your wings and clutch your things
  And then let go!

They have a million other games—
  Cloud-catching's one,
And mud-mixing after rain
  Is heaps and heaps of fun;
But when you go and stay with them
  Never mind the rest,
Take my advice—they're very nice,
  But steeple-sliding's best!

ROSE FYLEMAN

OVERHEARD ON A SALTMARSH

Nymph, nymph, what are your beads?
Green glass, goblin. Why do you stare at them?
Give them me.

No.

Give them me. Give them me.

No.

Then I will howl all night in the reeds,
Lie in the mud and howl for them.

Goblin, why do you love them so?

They are better than stars or water,
Better than voices of winds that sing,
Better than any man's fair daughter,
Your green glass beads on a silver ring.

Hush, I stole them out of the moon.

Give me your beads, I desire them.

No.

I will howl in a deep lagoon
For your green glass beads, I love them so.
Give them me. Give them.

No.

HAROLD MONRO

THE LITTLE ELF

I met a little Elf man, once,
Down where the lilies blow.
I asked him why he was so small,
And why he didn't grow.

He slightly frowned, and with his eye
He looked me through and through.
"I'm quite as big for me," said he,
"As you are big for you!"

JOHN KENDRICK BANGS

THE ELF AND THE DORMOUSE

Under a toadstool crept a wee Elf
Out of the rain to shelter himself.

Under the toadstool, sound asleep,
Sat a big Dormouse all in a heap.

Trembled the wee Elf, frightened, and yet
Fearing to fly away lest he get wet.

To the next shelter—maybe a mile!
Sudden the wee Elf smiled a wee smile.

Tugged till the toadstool toppled in two.
Holding it over him, gaily he flew.

Soon he was safe home, dry as could be.
Soon woke the Dormouse—"Good gracious me!

"Where is my toadstool?" loud he lamented
—And that's how umbrellas first were invented.

OLIVER HERFORD

SOME ONE

Some one came knocking
At my wee, small door;
Some one came knocking,
I'm sure—sure—sure;
I listened, I opened,
I looked to left and right,
But nought there was a-stirring
In the still dark night;
Only the busy beetle
Tap-tapping in the wall,
Only from the forest
The screech-owl's call,
Only the cricket whistling
While the dewdrops fall,
So I know not who came knocking,
At all, at all, at all.

WALTER DE LA MARE

More about everyday things

TOASTER TIME

Tick tick tick tick tick tick tick
Toast up a sandwich quick quick quick
Hamwich
Jamwich
Lick lick lick!

Tick tick tick tick tick tick—Stop!
POP!

EVE MERRIAM

CHOOSING

Which will you have, a ball or a cake?
A cake is so nice, yes, that's what I'll take.

Which will you have, a cake or a cat?
A cat is so soft, I think I'll take that.

Which will you have, a cat or a rose?
A rose is so sweet, I'll have that, I suppose.

Which will you have, a rose or a book?
A book full of pictures?—oh, do let me look!

ELEANOR FARJEON

THE CLOCK IN THE HALL

The clock in the hall
it strikes the hour
whether it's sunshine,
snow, or shower.

And when it is five-
past-nine each day,
it looks down on me
as if to say:

"Rain or sunshine!
sunshine or rain!
SUSANNA SIMPSON
IS LATE AGAIN!"

IVY O. EASTWICK

FERRY-BOATS

Over the river,
Over the bay,
Ferry-boats travel
Every day.

Most of the people
Crowd to the side
Just to enjoy
Their ferry-boat ride.

JAMES S. TIPPETT

BRIDGES

I like to look for bridges
Everywhere I go,
Where the cars go over
With water down below.

Standing by the railings
I watch the water slide
Smoothly under to the dark,
And out the other side.

RHODA BACMEISTER

RUDOLPH IS TIRED
OF THE CITY

These buildings are too close to me.
I'd like to PUSH away.
I'd like to live in the country.
And spread my arms all day.

I'd like to spread my breath out, too—
As farmers' sons and daughters do.

I'd tend the cows and chickens.
I'd do the other chores.
Then, all the hours left I'd go
A-SPREADING out-of-doors.

GWENDOLYN BROOKS

273

ENGINE

I wonder if the engine
That dashes down the track
Ever has a single thought
Of how it can get back.
With fifty cars behind it
And each car loaded full,
I wonder if it ever thinks
How hard it has to pull.
I guess it trusts the fireman;
It trusts the engineer;
I guess it knows the switchman
Will keep the tracks clear.

JAMES S. TIPPETT

274

SONG OF THE TRAIN

Clickety-clack,
Wheels on the track,
This is the way
They begin the attack:
Click-ety-clack,
Click-ety-clack,
Click-ety, *clack*-ety.
Click-ety
Clack.

Clickety-clack,
Over the crack,
Faster and faster
The song of the track:
Clickety-clack,
Clickety-clack,
Clickety, clackety,
Clackety
Clack.

Riding in front,
Riding in back,
Everyone hears
The song of the track:
Clickety-clack,
Clickety-clack,
Clickety, *clickety*,
Clackety
Clack.

DAVID MC CORD

THE MERRY-GO-ROUND

The merry-go-round
    whirls round and round
    in a giant circle on the ground.
And the horses run
    an exciting race
    while the wind blows music in your face.
Then the whole world spins
    to a colored tune
    but the ride is over much too soon.

MYRA COHN LIVINGSTON

THE SWING

How do you like to go up in a swing,
   Up in the air so blue?
Oh, I do think it the pleasantest thing
   Ever a child can do!

Up in the air and over the wall,
   Till I can see so wide,
Rivers and trees and cattle and all
   Over the countryside—

Till I look down on the garden green,
   Down on the roof so brown—
Up in the air I go flying again,
   Up in the air and down!

ROBERT LOUIS STEVENSON

THE LITTLE JUMPING GIRLS

Jump—jump—jump—
   Jump away
From this town into
   The next, today.

Jump—jump—jump
   Jump over the moon;
Jump all the morning
   And all the noon.

Jump—jump—jump—
   Jump all night;
Won't our mothers
   Be in a fright?

Jump—jump—jump—
   Over the sea;
What wonderful wonders
   We shall see.

Jump—jump—jump—
   Jump far away;
And all come home
   Some other day.

KATE GREENAWAY

SWIMMING

When all the days are hot and long
And robin bird has ceased his song,
I go swimming every day
And have the finest kind of play.

I've learned to dive and I can float
As easily as does a boat;
I splash and plunge and laugh and shout
Till Daddy tells me to come out.

It's much too soon; I'd like to cry
For I can see the ducks go by,
And Daddy Duck—how I love him—
He lets his children swim and swim!

I feel that I would be in luck
If I could only be a duck!

CLINTON SCOLLARD

277

WHEN I'M AN ASTRONAUT

When I'm myself,
It's "1, 2, 3,"
I count
As I've been taught.
But in my
Space suit—
"3, 2, 1,"
Says the astronaut.

LELAND B. JACOBS

BUMP ON MY KNEE

Look at the terrible bump
       on my knee
(I thought I was playing carefully,
   but the wheel turned round
   and I suddenly found
   myself on the ground)

It doesn't hurt terribly
   but I think
   I would like
   you to paint it
   a
   beautiful
   pink!

MYRA COHN LIVINGSTON

FIVE CHANTS *(First part)*

Every time I climb a tree
Every time I climb a tree
Every time I climb a tree
I scrape a leg
Or skin a knee
And every time I climb a tree
I find some ants
Or dodge a bee
And get the ants
All over me

And every time I climb a tree
Where have you been?
They say to me
But don't they know that I am free
Every time I climb a tree?
I like it best
To spot a nest
That has an egg
Or maybe three

And then I skin
The other leg
But every time I climb a tree
I see a lot of things to see
Swallows rooftops and TV
And all the fields and farms there be
Every time I climb a tree
Though climbing may be good for ants
It isn't awfully good for pants
But still it's pretty good for me
Every time I climb a tree

DAVID MC CORD

VERN

When walking in a tiny rain
Across the vacant lot,
A pup's a good companion—
If a pup you've got.

And when you've had a scold,
And no one loves you very,
And you cannot be merry,
A pup will let you look at him,
And even let you hold
His little wiggly warmness—

And let you snuggle down beside.
Nor mock the tears you have to hide.

GWENDOLYN BROOKS

RUBBER BOOTS

Little boots and big boots,
  Traveling together
On the shiny sidewalks,
  In the rainy weather,
Little boots and big boots,
  Oh, it must be fun
To splash the silver raindrops
  About you as you run,
Or scatter bits of rainbow
  Beneath the April sun!

Big boots and little boots,
  You know how it feels
To have the white clouds drifting
  Far below your heels;
And it is dizzy pleasure,
  Along the way to school,
To walk the lacy tree tops
  That lie in every pool.

Little boots and big boots,
  How you like to putter
In every slender streamlet
  That scampers down the gutter!

ROWENA BASTIN BENNETT

SPRING RAIN

The storm came up so very quick
  It couldn't have been quicker.
I should have brought my hat along,
  I should have brought my slicker.

My hair is wet, my feet are wet,
  I couldn't be much wetter.
I fell into a river once
  But this is even better.

MARCHETTE CHUTE

WASHING

What is all this washing about,
Every day, week in, week out?
From getting up till going to bed,
I'm tired of hearing the same thing said.

Whether I'm dirty or whether I'm not,
Whether the water is cold or hot,
Whether I like or whether I don't
Whether I will or whether I won't—
"Have you washed your hands, and washed
    your face?"
I seem to *live* in the washing-place.

Whenever I go for a walk or ride,
As soon as I put my nose inside
The door again, there's some one there
With a sponge and soap, and a lot they care
If I have something better to do,
"Now wash your face and your fingers too."

Before a meal is ever begun,
And after ever a meal is done,
It's time to turn on the waterspout.

Please, what *is* all this washing about?

JOHN DRINKWATER

Prayers

$\mathcal{P}salm$ 100

Make a joyful noise unto the Lord, all ye lands.
Serve the Lord with gladness:
Come before His presence with singing.

Know ye that the Lord He is God:
It is He that hath made us, and not we ourselves;
We are His people, and the sheep of His pasture.

Enter into His gates with thanksgiving,
And into His courts with praise:
Be thankful unto Him, and bless His name.

For the Lord is good;
His mercy is everlasting;
And His truth endureth to all generations.

THE BIBLE

Old Gaelic Lullaby

Hush! the waves are rolling in,
White with foam, white with foam.
Father toils amid the din,
But baby sleeps at home.

Hush! the winds roar hoarse and deep!
On they come, on they come!
Brother seeks the wandering sheep,
But baby sleeps at home.

Hush! the rain sweeps o'er the knowes
Where they roam, where they roam.
Sister goes to seek the cows,
But baby sleeps at home.

FATHER OF ALL

Father of all, in Heaven above,
We thank Thee for Thy love;
Our food, our home, and all we wear
Tell of Thy loving care.

THANK YOU

Thank You for the world so sweet,
Thank You for the food we eat,
Thank You for the birds that sing,
Thank You, God, for everything.

MRS. E. RUTTER LEATHAN

FATHER, WE THANK THEE

For flowers that bloom about our feet,
Father, we thank Thee,
For tender grass so fresh and sweet,
Father, we thank Thee,
For song of bird and hum of bee,
For all things fair we hear or see,
Father in heaven, we thank Thee.

For blue of stream and blue of sky,
Father, we thank Thee,
For pleasant shade of branches high,
Father, we thank Thee,
For fragrant air and cooling breeze,
For beauty of the blooming trees,
Father in heaven, we thank Thee.

AUTHOR UNKNOWN

FOR THIS NEW MORNING

For this new morning and its light,
For rest and shelter of the night,
For health and food, for love and friends,
For every gift His goodness sends
We thank Thee, gracious Lord. Amen.

FOR THE NIGHT

Father, we thank Thee for the night,
And for the pleasant morning light;
For rest and food and loving care,
And all that makes the day so fair.
Help us to do the things we should,
To be to others kind and good;
In all we do, all we say,
To grow more loving every day.

291

DEAR LORD,
FOR THESE
THREE THINGS
I PRAY

Dear Lord, for these three things I pray:
To know Thee more clearly,
To love Thee more dearly,
To follow Thee more nearly,
Every day.

VESPERS

Little Boy kneels at the foot of the bed,
Droops on the little hands little gold head.
Hush! Hush! Whisper who dares!
Christopher Robin is saying his prayers.

God bless Mummy. I know that's right.
Wasn't it fun in the bath tonight?
The cold's so cold, and the hot's so hot.
Oh! *God bless Daddy*—I quite forgot.

If I open my fingers a little bit more,
I can see Nanny's dressing gown on the door.
It's a beautiful blue, but it hasn't a hood.
Oh! *God bless Nanny and make her good.*

Mine has a hood, and I lie in bed,
And pull the hood right over my head,
And I shut my eyes, and I curl up small,
And nobody knows that I'm there at all.

Oh! *Thank you, God, for a lovely day.*
And what was the other I had to say?
I said, "Bless Daddy," so what can it be?
Oh! Now I remember it. *God bless Me.*

Little Boy kneels at the foot of the bed,
Droops on the little hands little gold head.
Hush! Hush! Whisper who dares!
Christopher Robin is saying his prayers.

A. A. MILNE

THE PRAYER
OF
THE LITTLE BIRD

Dear God,
I don't know how to pray by myself
very well,
but will You please
protect my little nest from wind and rain?
Put a great deal of dew on the flowers,
many seeds in my way.
Make Your blue very high,
Your branches lissom;
let Your kind light stay late in the sky
and set my heart brimming with such music
that I must sing, sing, sing. . . .
Please, Lord.

CARMEN BERNOS DE GASZTOLD
Translated by Rumer Godden

Poems
and
rhymes
set
to music

HEY, DIDDLE, DIDDLE

Lively

f

Hey, did - dle, did - dle, the cat and the fid - dle, the

cow jumped o - ver the moon;.............. The lit - tle dog laughed to

see such sport, and the dish ran a - way with the spoon..........

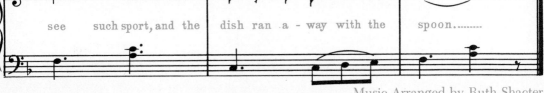

Music Arranged by Ruth Shacter

TWINKLE, TWINKLE, LITTLE STAR

Moderato

An Old French Air

mf

Twin-kle, twin-kle lit - tle star,

how I won-der what you are! Up a-bove the world so high,

like a dia-mond in the sky, Twin-kle, twin-kle lit - tle star,

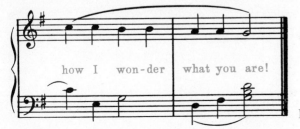

how I won-der what you are!

Music Arranged by Ruth Shacter

THE FARMER IN THE DELL

Allegro

The far-mer in the dell,......... the far-mer in the dell,...........

Heigh - ho, the der-ry-o, the far-mer in the dell................

Music Arranged by Ruth Shacter

LITTLE BO-PEEP

Gently

mp

Lit-tle Bo Peep has lost her sheep, and can't tell where to find them,

Leave them a-lone, and they'll come home Wag-ging their tails..... be - hind them.

Music Arranged by Ruth Shacter

BAA, BAA, BLACK SHEEP

Baa, Baa, black sheep, have you an-y wool?
Yes, sir! Yes, sir! three bags full.
One for my mas - ter, and one for my dame, And one for the lit - tle boy who lives down the lane.

Music Arranged by Ruth Shacter

OH, DEAR! WHAT CAN THE MATTER BE?

Con Moto

Words and Tune Traditional

Oh, Dear! what can the mat-ter be? Dear, Dear! what can the mat-ter be? Oh, Dear! what can the mat-ter be? John-ny's so long at the fair......

Fine

He prom-ised he'd buy me a fair-ing should please me, and then for a kiss, Oh he vowed he would tease me, He prom-ised to buy me a bunch of blue rib-bons to tie up my bon-nie brown hair..............

D.C. al Fine

Music Arranged by Ruth Shacter

THE MUFFIN MAN

Allegro

Words and Music Traditional

1.Oh do you know the Muf-fin man, the Muf-fin man, the Muf-fin man, Oh
2.Oh yes I know the Muf-fin man, the Muf-fin man, the Muf-fin man, Oh

do you know the Muf-fin man, who lives in Dru-ry lane?
yes I know the Muf-fin man, who lives in Dru-ry lane!

Music Arranged by Ruth Shacter

THREE BLIND MICE

Allegretto

Three blind mice,........ three blind mice,........ See how they run!........

See how they run!........... They all ran af-ter the farm-er's wife, who

cut off their tails with a carv-ing knife, Did you ev - er see such a

sight in your life as three blind mice?

Music Arranged by Ruth Shacter

HICKORY, DICKORY, DOCK!

Allegro

Words and Tune Traditional

Hick-o-ry, dick-o-ry dock! The mouse ran up the clock; The clock struck one, and the mouse ran down, Hick-o-ry, dick-o-ry dock!

Music Arranged by Ruth Shacter

JACK AND JILL

Moderato

Jack and Jill went up the hill to fetch a pail of wa-ter.

Jack fell down and broke his crown, and Jill came tum-bling af-ter.

Music Arranged by Ruth Shacter

SING A SONG OF SIXPENCE

Allegro

ff

1. Sing a song of six-pence, a pock-et full of rye.......

Four and twen-ty black-birds baked in-to a pie.......

When the pie was o-pened, the birds be-gan to sing.......

Was-n't that a dain-ty dish to set be-fore the King.......

Music Arranged by Ruth Shacter

2. The King was in his counting house counting out his money;
The Queen was in her parlor, eating bread and honey;
The maid was in the garden, hanging out the clothes,
Down came a blackbird and snapped off her nose.

FRÈRE JACQUES

Lively

An Old French Round

Frè - re Jac - ques, Frè - re Jac - ques, Dor - mez
Are you sleep - ing, Are you sleep - ing, Broth - er

vous? Dor - mez vous? Son - nez les ma - ti - nes:
John? Broth-er John? Morn-ing bells are ring - ing:

Son-nez les ma - ti - nes: Din, Don, Din, Din, Don, Din.
Morn-ing bells are ring - ing: Ding, Dong Ding, Ding, Dong Ding.

Music Arranged by Ruth Shacter

ROW, ROW, ROW YOUR BOAT

Rocking motion

Row, Row, Row your boat, gent - ly down the stream,

Mer-ri-ly mer-ri-ly, mer-ri-ly, mer-ri-ly, Life is but a dream.

Music Arranged by Ruth Shacter

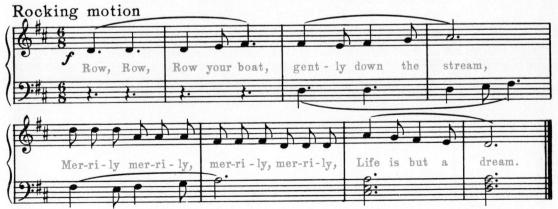

ALL THROUGH THE NIGHT

Softly

A Traditional Welsh Air

Sleep, my child, and peace at-tend thee, All through the night;

Guard-ian an-gels God will send thee, All through the night,

Soft the drow-sy hours are creep-ing, Hill and vale in slum-ber

steep-ing, I my lov-ing vig-il keep-ing, All through the night.

Music Arranged by Ruth Shacter

HUSH, MY BABY

A Traditional American Lullaby

Gently

p

1. Hush, li'l ba - by, don't say a word,

Dad - dy -'ll buy you a mock - ing bird.

Music Arranged by Ruth Shacter

2. When that mockingbird won't sing,
Daddy'll buy you a diamond ring.

3. When that diamond ring turns to brass,
Daddy'll buy you a looking glass.

4. When that looking glass gets broke,
Daddy'll buy you a billy goat.

5. When that billy goat gets bony,
Daddy'll buy you a Shetland pony.

6. When that pony runs away,
Ta-ra-ra-ra-boom-de-ay.

Illustration Acknowledgments

The publishers of *Childcraft* gratefully acknowledge the following artists, photographers, publishers, agencies, and corporations for illustrations in this volume. Page numbers refer to two-page spreads. The words *"(left),"* *"(center),"* *"(top),"* *"(bottom),"* and *"(right),"* indicate position on the spread. All illustrations are the exclusive property of the publishers of *Childcraft* unless names are marked with an asterisk (*).

1: Robert Keys
8-9: Sylvia Sullivan
10-11: Nancy Burkert
12-13: Tom diGrazia
14-15: Sally Augustiny
16-17: *(left)* Susan Perl; *(top right)* Susan Perl; *(bottom right)* Marie Hall Ets
18-19: Christine Westerberg
20-21: Marc Simont
22-23: Gerber Products Company *
24-25: *(top)* Fred Meyer; *(bottom)* Suzi Hawes
26-27: Evaline Ness
28-29: Fred Meyer
30-31: *(left)* Walter Chandoha *; *(right)* Elizabeth Schon
32-33: Vernon McKissack
34-35: Garth Williams
36-37: *(left)* Russell Jackson; *(right)* Russell Jackson, Dept. of Conservation, State of Indiana *
38-39: Susan Perl
40-41: *(left)* Henry C. Pitz; *(right)* Leonard Weisgard
42-43: art, Robert Kresin; photo, Mel Kaspar
44-45: Uri Shulevitz
46-47: Gyo Fujikawa
48-49: Leonard Weisgard
50-51: art, Eloise Wilkin; photo, Erika Schmachtenberger, Bildberichterstattung, *Deutschland Revue* *
52-53: *(left)* Phiz Mezey; *(right)* Russell Jackson
54-55: Mary Horton
56-57: Charles Reiche, Scope Associates *
58-59: Mary Horton
60-61: art, Mary Horton; photo, Douglas Kirkland *
62-63: *(left)* Mary Horton; *(right)* Frank Fenner
64-65: Dev Appleyard *
66-67: *(left)* Thomas Handforth; *(right)* Robert McCloskey
68-69: F.P.G. *
70-71: art, Gordon Kwiatkowski; photo, Dorothy McLaughlin *
72-73: Feodor Rojankovsky
74-75: William Steig
76-77: photo, Yerkes Observatory *; art, Mary Horton
78-79: Nicolas Mordvinoff
80-81: Mary Horton
82-83: *(left, top and bottom right)* from *The Shadow Book* by Beatrice Schenk de Regniers *,

photographs © 1960 by Isabel Gordon, reproduced by permission of Harcourt, Brace & World, Inc. *; *(center)* Alfred Eisenstaedt, *Life,* © Time Inc. *
84-85: Art Kane *
86-87: Angela Adams
88-89: Rosi Marie Bednarik-Gaigg
90-91: Berta and Elmer Hader; *Childcraft* photo
92-93: *(left)* Carroll Seghers II, © The Cream of Wheat Corp. *; *(right)* Eloise Wilkin
94-95: *(left)* Katherine Milhous; *(right)* John Henry
96-97: Mary Miller Salem
98-99: *(left)* Cole, Monkmeyer *; *(right)* Susan Perl
100-101: *(left)* Dick Smith *; *(right)* Russell Jackson
102-103: *(left)* Walt Langenberg, *U.S. Camera* *; *(right)* Walter Chandoha *
104-105: *(left)* Gordon Laite; *(right)* Gene Daniels, Black Star *
106-107: Fred Womack
108-109: *(left)* Mary Hauge; *(right)* Garth Williams
110-111: *(top)* Garth Williams; *(bottom)* Vernon McKissack
112-113: *(left)* Grant Heilman *; *(right)* Neal Cochran
114-115: art, Clark Bruorton; photography, Frank Cassidy
116-117: Gordon Laite
118-119: Garth Williams
120-121: *(left)* Vernon McKissack; *(right)* H. Armstrong Roberts *
122-123: Gyo Fujikawa
124-125: *(left)* Eraldo Carugati; *(right)* H. A. Aldridge
126-127: *(left)* *Childcraft* photo; *(right)* Russell Jackson
128-129: Trina Hyman
130-131: Susan Perl
132-133: Meg Wohlberg
134-135: Joseph Veno
136-137: photography, Mel Kaspar; art, Clark Bruorton
138-139: Dora Leder
140-141: *(left)* Mary Horton; *(right)* Alaine Johnson *
142-143: Mary Horton
144-145: *(left)* painting "La Toilette" by Mary Cassatt, The Art Institute of Chicago *; *(right)* Clark Bruorton
146-147: Maude Petersham
148-149: *(left)* Michael Eagle; *(right)* Russell Jackson
150-151: *(left)* Phiz Mezey; *(right)* Maurice Sendak
152-153: *(left)* Leigh Grant; *(right)* Mia Carpenter, Joseph Love Inc. *

Author Index

Use this index to find a poem if you know only the name of the author. You can also find a poem by using the Title Index on page 312, the First-Line Index on page 316, and the Subject Index on page 318. In addition, the General Index in Volume 15 is a key to all the books.

Shapiro, Arnold L.
  I Speak, I Say, I Talk,
    228
Sherman, Frank Dempster
  Snowbird, The, 63
Shiki
  haiku: *What a*
    wonderful, 211
Stephens, James
  Breakfast Time, 143
  Check, 74
Stevenson, Robert Louis
  Autumn Fires, 60
  Bed in Summer, 59
  Cow, The, 113
  Land of Counterpane,
    The, 170
  Little Land, The, 221
  My Shadow, 82
  Rain, 91
  Singing, 95
  Swing, The, 277
  Time To Rise, 143
  Where Go the Boats?,
    210
  Wind, The, 84
Stiles, L. J.
  Growing, 143
Swett, Susan Hartley
  July, 68

Taylor, Jane
  Little Pussy, 103
  Twinkle, Twinkle, Little
    Star, 77, 297

Teasdale, Sara
  April, 66
  Falling Star, The, 76
  February Twilight, 66
Thompson, Dorothy Brown
  Bigger, 112
  Maps, 196
Tietjens, Eunice
  Moving, 130
  Thaw, 99
Tippett, James S.
  Building a Skyscraper,
    212
  Engine, 274
  Ferry-Boats, 271
  "Sh," 155
  Sleet Storm, 98
  Up in the Air, 196
Turner, Nancy Byrd
  Spring Wind, 55
  When Young Melissa
    Sweeps, 133
  Wind Capers, 85
  Wings and Wheels, 170

unknown
  All Through the Night,
    306
  Chick, Chick,
    Chatterman, 34
  Dear Lord, for These
    Three Things I Pray,
    292
  Down with the Lambs,
    52

unknown *(continued)*
  Dream Party, A, 148
  Farmer in the Dell, The,
    298
  Father of All, 288
  Father, We Thank Thee,
    291
  Fishy-Fishy in the
    Brook, 37
  For the Night, 291
  For This New Morning,
    291
  Frère Jacques, 305
  Had a Mule, 15
  Hickory, Dickory, Dock!,
    303
  Hush, Little Baby, 10,
    307
  I Had a Cow, 36
  I Know a Man, 41
  I Saw a Ship A-Sailing,
    238
  It's Raining, It's
    Pouring, 51
  Light-Hearted Fairy,
    The, 262
  Mr. Nobody, 243
  Muffin Man, The, 301
  Oh, Dear! What Can the
    Matter Be?, 300
  Old Christmas
    Greeting, 72
  Old Gaelic Lullaby, 287
  Postman, The, 190
  Rain, Rain, Go Away, 91

unknown *(continued)*
  Row, Row, Row Your
    Boat, 305
  Seven Blackbirds in a
    Tree, 17
  Song of the Frog, The,
    148
  Spring, 54
  Sweeter Than Sugar,
    11
  This Little Pig Went to
    Market, 17
  Three Blind Mice, 302
  We Are All Nodding,
    23
  Whisky Frisky, 108
Untermeyer, Jean Starr
  Glimpse in Autumn, 70

Welles, Winifred
  Dogs and Weather, 104
Willson, Dixie
  Mist and All, The, 62
Wolfe, Ffrida
  Choosing Shoes, 139
Worth, Kathryn
  Smells, 151
Wynne, Annette
  Indian Children, 199
  Letter Is A Gypsy Elf,
    A, 217
  Telegraph, The, 216

Young, Barbara
  Road Fellows, 233

Title Index

Use this index to find a poem if you know only the title of the poem. You can also find a poem by using the Author Index on page 310, the First-Line Index on page 316, and the Subject Index on page 318. In addition, the General Index in Volume 15 is a key to all the books.

314

First-Line Index

Use this index to find a poem if you know only the first line of the poem. You can also find a poem by using the Author Index on page 310, the Title Index on page 312, and the Subject Index on page 318. In addition, the General Index in Volume 15 is a key to all the books.

Subject Index

Use this index if you want to find a poem about a particular subject. You can also find a poem by using the Author Index on page 310, the Title Index on page 312, and the First-Line Index on page 316. In addition, the General Index in Volume 15 is a key to all the books.

320